LOCKE'S

CONDUCT

OF THE

UNDERSTANDING

EDITED

WITH INTRODUCTION, NOTES, ETC.

BY

THOMAS FOWLER, D.D.

President of Corpus Christi College, and formerly Professor of Logic
in the University of Oxford; Honorary Doctor of Laws
in the University of Edinburgh

Fifth Edition

OXFORD

AT THE CLARENDON PRESS

1901

PRINTED IN ENGLAND
AT THE OXFORD UNIVERSITY PRESS

PREFACE.

LOCKE'S tract or rather chapter 'Of the Conduct of the Understanding,' though often praised, and occasionally republished in a separate form, has never been edited with notes. It is thought that such assistance as is offered to the student in this edition may cause it to be more widely read and more generally useful.

The testimony accorded to this book by Hallam, in his Introduction to the Literature of Europe, may fittingly occupy a position in its editor's preface :—

'I cannot think any parent or instructor justified in neglecting to put this little treatise in the hands of a boy about the time when the reasoning faculties become developed. It will give him a sober and serious, not flippant or self-conceited, independency of thinking ; and, while it teaches how to distrust ourselves and to watch those prejudices which necessarily grow up from one cause or another, will inspire a reasonable confidence in what he has well considered, by taking off a little of that deference to authority which is the more to be regretted in its excess that, like its cousin-german, party-spirit, it is frequently united to loyalty of heart and the generous enthusiasm of youth.'

The treatise is unrevised and incomplete, but these circumstances (the reasons of which are explained in the Introduction) only slightly affect its value to the student.

It may be remarked that the punctuation of the original edition, which seems to have been made almost entirely at hap-hazard, has been revised throughout by the present editor.

The sketch of Locke's life prefixed to this work is necessarily meagre. For a fuller biography and an account of his writings generally, the reader is referred to the editor's 'Locke,' recently published by Messrs. Macmillan in their series of 'English Men of Letters,' or to the elaborate and, so far as concerns the biographical portion, almost exhaustive Life of Locke by Mr. Fox-Bourne in two volumes.

₊ Words obelized, thus, † †, occur in the original text, but require to be omitted, in order to make sense. Words within brackets, thus, [ ], do not occur in the original text, but require to be inserted, in order to make sense. Both these signs have been used as sparingly as possible.

LINCOLN COLLEGE,
Nov. 5, 1880.

CONTENTS.

INTRODUCTION.

JOHN LOCKE, who is now best known as a philosopher, though, in his own time, he was almost equally celebrated as a theologian, financier, and statesman, was born at Wrington, a village in the North of Somersetshire, not far from Bristol, Aug. 29, 1632. His family, who belonged to the lower class of English gentry, were in tolerably comfortable circumstances, and to the judicious care of his father young Locke seems to have been indebted for many of his characteristics, both moral and mental. Of his early boyhood we learn next to nothing, except that it pretty nearly coincided with the troubles of the Civil Wars. 'I no sooner perceived myself in the world,' he wrote in 1660, 'but I found myself in a storm which has lasted almost hitherto.' It was probably in 1646 that he was admitted, under the stern government of Dr. Busby, a scholar of Westminster School. In the 'Thoughts concerning Education,' where he criticises most severely the discipline, methods, and studies of the English public-schools, there are probably many passages inspired by a recollection of his own experiences as a school-boy. In the Michaelmas Term of 1652, at what was then the rather late age of twenty, Locke commenced residence in Oxford as a Student of Christ Church. There he took his degrees, and became in due time Tutor and Censor. Probably the most powerful influence, which he underwent in Oxford, was that of Dr. John Owen, then Dean of Christ Church, a learned and, for those days, remarkably tolerant divine, who ranged himself on the side of the Independents. It has been suggested, with some plausibility, that the views subsequently embodied in

b

Locke's Letters on Toleration may partly have had their origin in the example and teaching of Owen.

Locke's first introduction to public life was as secretary to Sir Walter Vane in his mission to the Elector of Brandenburg, in 1665-6. The mission came to nothing, but Locke's notes on the manners, customs, and sights of Cleves, a quaint old town, then one of the residences of the Elector, are still full of a curious interest. He is peculiarly sarcastic on the scholastic disputations of the monks, but abounds in admiration for the mutual toleration shown, in private life, by the different religious sects. In the summer of 1666, some months after his return to England, he made an acquaintance at Oxford, which probably determined the future course of his life by diverting him from the quiet pursuits and studies of the University to politics and public business. The famous Lord Ashley, afterwards First Earl of Shaftesbury, had come to Oxford, for the purpose of drinking the Astrop waters, and the duty of providing them had been entrusted by Dr. David Thomas, Ashley's Oxford physician, to Locke, who was himself preparing for a medical career. There having been some miscarriage, Locke waited on Lord Ashley, to excuse the delay. Each was much pleased with the conversation of the other, and thus began a friendship which, whether in prosperity or adversity, seems never to have cooled during the remainder of their joint lives. In the summer of 1667, Locke took up his residence with Lord Ashley in London, though he still paid occasional visits of some length to Oxford. At Lord Ashley's town-house he formed the acquaintance of many men of letters and science, as well as of some of the leading politicians, then residing in London. At the same time, he was quietly pursuing his studies in medicine, politics, and philosophy. Besides acting as general adviser and medical attendant to Lord Ashley and his family, he was specially charged with the tuition of Anthony Ashley, the eldest son, who subsequently became Second Earl of Shaftesbury. It is curious that Locke afterwards stood in a similar relation, though rather as supervisor of studies than actual instructor, to the Third Earl of Shaftesbury, son of the second and grandson of the First Earl, the famous author of the Characteristics. While living in Lord Ashley's house, and acting, in a sort of informal capacity, as secretary to the 'lords proprietors of the colony of Carolina,' of whom Ashley was one, he drew up the document, now printed in his works, called 'The Fundamental Constitutions of Carolina.' Some of the provisions, however, must have been decidedly distasteful to Locke, and we must by no means regard him as responsible for the scheme in its final shape. But a far more important work, the famous Essay on the Human Understanding, seems to have had its first origin about or soon after the same period. We are told, in his Epistle to the Reader, that five or six friends meeting at his chamber, 'and discoursing on a subject very remote from this, found themselves quickly at a stand by the difficulties that rose on every side.' After they had puzzled themselves for some time, without coming any nearer to a resolution of their doubts, it came into his thoughts that they took a wrong course, 'and that, before we set ourselves upon enquiries of that nature, it was necessary to examine our own abilities, and see what objects our Understandings were or were not fitted to deal with.' This course he proposed to the company, and 'it was thereupon agreed that this should be our first enquiry.' 'Some hasty and undigested thoughts on a subject I had never before considered, which I set down against our next meeting, gave the first entrance into this discourse, which, having been thus begun by chance, was continued by entreaty; written by incoherent parcels; and, after long intervals of neglect, resumed again, as my humour or occasions permitted; and, at last, in a retirement where an attendance on my health gave me leisure, it was brought into that order thou now seest it.' The Copy of the First Edition of the Essay which belonged to Sir James Tyrrell, one of Locke's most intimate friends, is now in the British Museum. In it is a marginal note, stating that the discussion on the occasion alluded to turned on 'the principles of morality and revealed religion.' It is also stated that the time was the winter of 1673. The latter statement, however, is probably mistaken, as there is concurrent evidence to show that it was in 1670 or 1671. It would thus appear that Locke was occupied nearly twenty years in maturing the greatest of his works ; for the Essay was not published till 1690.

In November, 1672, Lord Ashley, who had recently been created Earl of Shaftesbury, was appointed Lord High Chancellor of England. Locke shared to some extent in his patron's good fortune, being made Secretary of Presentations, that is, of the Chancellor's Church Patronage, and subsequently Secretary to the Council of Trade and Foreign Plantations. The salary of the latter office, however, he appears never to have received. But his circumstances were always easy, and, being neither needy nor avaricious, he was entirely free from the sordid cares which often consume so much of the time and thoughts of men of letters.

One care, however, he constantly had. His health was always extremely weak, and the air of London seems to have been peculiarly trying to it. The malady from which he mainly suffered was a bronchial affection, which compelled him in 1675 to seek what was then the usual resort of English invalids, Montpellier. There, at Paris, and in making excursions in the country parts of France, he spent his time till the spring of 1679, when he returned to England. While Locke was living abroad, Shaftesbury had been imprisoned in the Tower for a year, but, by a sudden turn of fortune, he had been restored to office as President of the newly created Council. What were Locke's exact relations to Shaftesbury during this second tenure of office, we do not know, but any way the two friends were in close and frequent intercourse. In the autumn, however, of this year, the King felt himself strong enough to assert his own predilections, and Shaftesbury's name was, 'by his Majesty's command in Council,' struck out of the list of the Privy Council. Locke, like a true man, adhered to the cause of his patron, even in adversity, and we never obtain the slightest glimpse of any attempt to make terms with the party in power on his own account. One of his main cares at this time was the superintendence of the education of Shaftesbury's grandson, afterwards the third earl, who, the second earl being apparently a person of somewhat feeble intellect, had been made over to the formal guardianship of his grandfather. The author of the Characteristics, though an opponent of Locke's philosophy, always acknowledges the deepest gratitude for the care which he had bestowed on him in childhood and youth. During these years, political animosities were growing more and more bitter, and political intrigues more and more complicated, till, at last, the state of the kingdom became exceedingly critical. We can hardly be surprised that, when both sides seemed ready to strike, ministers took the initiative. On the 2nd of July, 1681, Shaftesbury was arrested on a charge of High Treason, and committed to the Tower. When he was at length brought to trial, the Grand Jury, amidst the plaudits of the spectators, threw out the Bill. But both his political and natural life were drawing to a close. In the summer of 1682, he began to concert measures with Monmouth, Russell, and others, for a general rising against the King. The plot was soon discovered, and, after hiding for some time in England, he escaped to Holland, where he died of gout in the stomach, Jan. 21, 1682-3.

Though there is no evidence to implicate Locke in Shaftesbury's conspiracy, and though it is most improbable that he was engaged in the plots which succeeded it, enough suspicion attached to him to render his residence in England highly dangerous. He escaped to Holland in the autumn of 1683, and remained there, in what was, on the whole, a very pleasant, and certainly a very profitable exile, till the occurrence of the English Revolution. With the exception of some months during which he was obliged to hide for his life or, at least, to go through the ceremony of hiding for it, in consequence of demands from the English court, his surroundings seem to have been as comfortable and congenial as they could well be. He made many friendships, including those of the theologian, Limborch, and the philosopher and critic, Le Clerc. And his leisure was sufficient to enable him, not only to complete the Essay on the Human Understanding, but also to write the Letter on Toleration, the Thoughts concerning Education, and the second of the two Treatises on Government, none of which, however, were published till after his return to England. But, though he was mainly engaged in study and writing, his political interests and activities had by no means flagged. Locke took a principal share in the negotiations which placed William of Orange on the throne of England, and, when he returned to his own country, it was in the company of the Princess Mary, William's Queen. One incident of his exile ought not to be omitted, though, perhaps, his biographers have made too much of it. Soon after his retreat to Holland, and in consequence of his being suspected of writing political pamphlets, he was deprived, by order of the government, of his Studentship at Christ Church. The responsibility of this act attaches to the Ministry and not to the Dean and Chapter of Christ Church, for, the College being a royal foundation, it was then held that the Crown had an absolute right to appoint or suspend members on the foundation at its pleasure. And, though the Dean and Chapter might have won our admiration, had they, at the risk of their places, resisted the royal commands, like the Fellows of Magdalen College in the next reign, they can hardly be blamed for not having exhibited so extraordinary a spirit of heroism. It may be mentioned, as an instance of Locke's magnanimity, that he desisted from an appeal for restitution, made after the Revolution, out of consideration for the existing possessor.

On his return to England, in 1688-9, Locke was almost immediately offered the important diplomatic post of ambassador to Frederick the Great, Elector of Brandenburg, but, on the ground of his feeble health, he was compelled to decline it. His health, which seems to have suffered from his return to England, and especially from 'the pestilent smoke of the metropolis' (malignus hujus urbis fumus), was henceforth an object of constant solicitude to him. He often made prolonged visits to the houses of his friends in the country, but, at last, in the spring of 1691, he entered into an arrangement with Sir Francis and Lady Masham, by which he was able to regard their manor-house of Oates, near High Laver in Essex, as his permanent home. Oates is in a pleasant country, abounding in wood and water, and Locke, 'having made trial of the air of the place, thought none would be more suitable to him.' Lady Masham, who was daughter of Dr. Ralph Cudworth, the metaphysician and moralist, best known to us as the author of the 'Treatise concerning Eternal and Immutable Morality,' had, as Damaris Cudworth, been one of Locke's acquaintances, before his retirement to Holland. She and her step-daughter, Esther Masham, devoted themselves to him for the remainder of his life, and nothing can be more touching than the mutual esteem and affection, never broken, apparently, by the slightest jealousy or ill-feeling, which henceforth marked his relations with the whole of the Masham family. No philosopher, probably, ever enjoyed a more congenial retreat, or had the good fortune to be tended in his later years with more care and solicitude.

About a year before his settlement at Oates, Locke had brought out his great work, the Essay on the Human Understanding, the main topics of which, as we have already seen, had suggested themselves to him about twenty years before. For the copyright of this book, the most important treatise, and that which has exercised the greatest and widest influence, in the whole range of English philosophy, he received the sum of £30. In the spring of 1689, had appeared, at Gouda in Holland, the Epistola de Tolerantia, in which he boldly maintained that the civil magistrate has no concern with religious worship or doctrine, except so far as it may affect the security of civil government. The exception, Locke conceived, excluded Atheists, Roman Catholics, and perhaps certain sects of Antinomians. This tract, which was soon translated into English, was brought out, without Locke's name and apparently without his knowledge, by Limborch, to whom it had been addressed as a letter.

If we except some congratulatory verses, presented by Oxford students to Cromwell in the 'Musarum Oxoniensium ἐλαιοφορία,' which was published, while he was an Under-graduate, in 1654, Locke, active as his pen had been all along, made no appearance in print till he was nearly fifty-four years of age. Such was his natural modesty that, had it not been for the fortunate circumstances which brought him into contact with Le Clerc, the editor of the Bibliothèque Universelle, he might never have consented to make any of his writings public. In the number of the Review just mentioned for July, 1686, appeared Locke's Method of a Common-Place Book, under the title 'Méthode Nouvelle de dresser des Re-cueils,' and, in the number for January, 1687–8, an epitome of the Essay, which seems to have been then completed, was translated into French by Le Clerc. After his return to England, his works followed one another in rapid succession, though they generally appeared anonymously. Thus, besides the Epistola de Tolerantia and the Essay, there were pub-lished, within a year or two of his return, the Two Treatises of Government (designed to defend the principles of the Revolu-tion), and the Second Letter concerning Toleration. In 1692 appeared the Third Letter for Toleration (Locke, not-withstanding his peaceful disposition, had now been forced into an embittered controversy), and a financial tract, of which I shall say more presently, entitled 'Some Considera-tions of the Lowering of Interest and Raising the Value of Money.' In the following year, he published, in the form of a Treatise, several letters on Education which he had written, during his stay in Holland, to his friend Edward Clarke of Chipley. These 'Thoughts concerning Education' touch on some of the same topics as the treatise here re-published on 'The Conduct of the Understanding,' and the two might ad-vantageously be read together. Much of the earlier portion of the work, relating, as it does, to diet and physical manage-ment, is rather tedious and antiquated. But the criticisms on

what were then the main ingredients of a public-school education, theme-writing, verse-writing, repetition, and grammar,
and on the irrational severity which marked the scholastic
discipline of that time, may still be read with interest, perhaps even with profit.

Though Locke had refused diplomatic employment, he was
frequently consulted by the government and contributed
often very largely to the various political measures which
were passed during William's reign. Thus, he probably took
a considerable share in settling the terms of the Toleration
Act of 1689, though the 'small beginnings,' as he calls them,
of that act by no means satisfied his ideal of religious liberty.
Another order of questions which greatly interested him, and
towards the solution of which he probably contributed more
than any other man of that generation, was connected with
the monetary and financial difficulties which specially embar-
rassed William the Third's government during its earlier years.
It had been proposed to lower the maximum rate of interest,
allowed by law, from six per cent. to four, with the mistaken
idea that the trade of the country would, by this means, be
improved. It had also been proposed to remedy the very
serious evils under which the country was suffering from the
clipped coinage by 'raising the value,' as it was called, or, in
other words, lowering the denomination of the silver coins.
Both these schemes were opposed by Locke in the tract just
referred to, which was dedicated to Somers, an old friend of
his, now rapidly becoming one of the most powerful of
William the Third's ministers. Two other tracts on the
latter of these subjects followed in 1695. But Locke did not
content himself simply with opposing the schemes of others.
The re-coinage bill which received the Royal Assent on the
21st of January, 1695-6, and which, in spite of some tem-.
porary inconvenience, established the silver coinage once for
all on a satisfactory basis, had been shaped, to a great extent,
by his suggestions, and its passage through the two Houses
was largely facilitated by his exertions. The country soon
got rid of its clipped money, then the bane of all commerce,

and individuals lost comparatively little by the transition to a sound currency. Only a few months before the re-coinage bill was introduced, Locke had, it is said, drawn up the paper of Reasons by which the Commons induced the Lords to agree to the Repeal of the Licensing Act, thus effecting for the liberty of the press and the diffusion of literature what, as Macaulay says, 'Milton's Areopagitica had failed to do.' In connection with these topics, it may be mentioned that he was one of the original proprietors of the Bank of England, which, in spite of much Tory opposition, was established by Act of Parliament in the spring of 1694.

Soon after his return to England, Locke was appointed a Commissioner of Appeals, an office with a modest salary and very slight duties. In 1696, however, his services were enlisted for a far more arduous and important post. The government of William, of which Montague and Somers were now the most active members, determined to revive the old Council of Trade and Plantations. The duties of this commission were of the most multifarious character, comprising at once the administration of the colonies, of the poor-laws, and of the whole trade, internal and external, of the country. Locke very unwillingly accepted a place on the Council, but, having once consented to serve, he became its presiding genius. Whether in town or at Oates, he was always striking out new schemes, or working assiduously at the details of the department. For a little more than four years he devoted himself to this employment, conjointly, of course, with his literary work, but at last, in the summer of 1700, he was compelled, notwithstanding the remonstrances of the King, to resign his place at the board, in which it is interesting to know that he was succeeded by Matthew Prior, the poet.

During these years of public employment, Locke's pen was by no means idle. In 1695 had appeared his 'Reasonableness of Christianity,' a work in which, while assuming the infallibility of the Scriptures and the supernatural character of Christ's mission, he attempts to limit as far as possible the essential articles of the Christian faith. The views of religion and religious controversy adopted in this book have a general affinity with those of the Arminian or Remonstrant divines, among whom Locke had mixed in Holland. But, in some particulars, they approach the doctrines of Faustus Socinus, and hence a cry of Socinianism was not unnaturally raised against the author, who, though the work was published anonymously, was soon known to be Locke. The attack was commenced by a Cambridge clergyman named John Edwards, and for some years Locke was engaged in a bitter controversy both with him and with Stillingfleet, Bishop of Worcester, who endeavoured to excite theological prejudices against many passages in the Essay. Polemics of this character, so fashionable in that age, were against the whole bent of Locke's nature, and we may be certain that he was forced to take part in them most unwillingly. A far more congenial employment was the preparation of the Fourth Edition of the Essay, which, incorporating many additions and corrections, was issued in the autumn of 1699, and was the last published during its author's life-time. The tractate here re-published, on the Conduct of the Understanding, was designed to form a chapter in this new edition, but it seems to have grown so much on its author's hands, that he reserved it either for the next edition or for separate publication. The only other literary work of any importance, apart from controversial pamphlets, which occupied Locke's later years was the paraphrase and commentary on some of St. Paul's Epistles. He appears to have undertaken this work more for his own satisfaction, and as a kind of religious exercise in which he might spend his declining years, than with the view of instructing the public. These notes, which were not published till after his death, abound in good sense, but, as we might expect from the time at which they were written, they have little critical value.

After his resignation of his place on the Board of Trade, Locke seems to have lived a peculiarly quiet, and, at the same time, notwithstanding the increasing feebleness of his health, a peculiarly happy life. His cheerfulness and gaiety of temper never deserted him. The Mashams were indefatigable in their attention to all his wants, whether physical or intellectual. And, Oates being only about twenty miles from London, he was entertained by a constant flow of visitors. Amongst those who came down to see him, on single occasions, were Newton, the famous Earl of Peterborough, and William Molyneux, a clever and patriotic Member of the Irish House of Commons, with whom he had corresponded in familiar terms on a great variety of subjects for many years, but whom he had never before seen. The most constant visitor to Oates, however, was Peter King, a young kinsman of his own, who, having been taken out of his father's shop at Exeter by Locke, had been educated at Leyden, and was now rising rapidly at the English bar. King, who was an admirable lawyer, though not a brilliant speaker, afterwards became successively Recorder of London, Lord Chief Justice of the Common Pleas, and Lord High Chancellor of England. It is to his great-grandson, Peter, the seventh Lord King, father of the present Earl of Lovelace, that we owe the biography, which, previously to the publication of Mr. Fox-Bourne's Life, was the great authority for Locke's personal history. There seems to have been a strong mutual regard between the two cousins (King was Locke's first cousin once removed), and there can be no doubt that King owed his professional advancement to his elder relative, who not only introduced him to the bar but procured for him a seat in Parliament. When Locke died, the greater part of his property was divided between Peter King and Frank Masham, the son of Sir Francis and Lady Masham, who, like King, was a kind of adopted child. One of Locke's main characteristics was the attraction he always exercised on young people, and the kindness and consideration which he always showed to them.

The winter of 1703–4 seems to have aggravated the symptoms of his disease, and the return of summer did not bring its usual relief. He lingered on, however, during the autumn, retaining his faculties and his cheerfulness to the last. On the afternoon of the 28th of October, 1704, he passed quietly away, Lady Masham reading the Psalms to him almost up to the moment of his death. He is buried in the church-yard of High Laver. The epitaph on the wall above his tomb was composed by himself.

Locke's character was a peculiarly amiable one. He was eminently cheerful, kindly, and good-natured. With children and young people he was always an especial favourite. Few men of letters probably have possessed so much geniality combined with so much humour. He had rare powers of conversation, and was always acceptable in companies of all ranks, ages, and professions. Whatever the pursuit of the person he was conversing with, he had a happy knack of interesting himself in it, and was usually able to impart as well as receive information, whatever might be the subject of discourse. Hence, perhaps, the singular power of illustration and exposition which marks his works. He always writes like a man of the world, who draws from a varied stock of knowledge not of books only but of men. Another trait which distinguishes both his writings and his life is his transparent candour and his simple love of truth. The words of the epitaph which he designed for himself—'Literis innutritus eousque tantum profecit, ut veritati unice litaret' (Brought up among letters, he advanced just so far as to make an acceptable offering to truth alone)—well explain the main character and purpose of his career.

The treatise Of the Conduct of the Understanding, here re-published, was, as I have already stated, originally designed as an additional chapter to the Essay. Writing to William Molyneux, April 10, 1697, Locke himself gives the following account of the occasion of his writing on the subject. 'I have lately got a little leisure to think of some additions to my book, against the next edition, and within these few days have fallen upon a subject, that I know not how far it will lead me. I have written several pages on it, but the matter, the farther I go, opens the more upon me, and I cannot yet get sight of any end of it. The title of the chapter will be "Of the Conduct of the Understanding," which if I shall pursue as far as I imagine it will reach, and as it deserves, will, I conclude, make the largest chapter of my Essay.' The chapter did not, however, appear in the Fourth Edition of the Essay, nor was it published, or even revised, during its author's life-time. It was included in the 'Posthumous Works of Mr. John Locke,' edited anonymously, though probably by Peter King, in 1706. Of these treatises generally the editor says that 'for the greatest part they received not the author's last hand, being in a great measure little more than sudden views, intended to be afterwards revised and farther looked into, but by sickness, intervention of business, or preferable enquiries, happened to be thrust aside, and so lay neglected.' The account given of this treatise in particular will help to explain some of its peculiarities and defects :

'The Conduct of the Understanding he' (the Author) 'always thought to be a subject very well worth consideration. As any miscarriages in that point accidentally came into his mind, he used sometimes to set them down in writing, with those remedies he could then think of. This method, though it makes not that haste to the end which one would wish, is yet perhaps the only one that can be followed in the case ; it being here, as in physic, impossible for a physician to describe a disease, or seek remedies for it, till he comes to meet with it. Such particulars of this kind as occurred to the author at a time of leisure he set down in writing, intending, if he had lived, to have reduced them into order and method, and to have made a complete treatise ; whereas now it is only a collection of casual observations, sufficient to make men see some faults in the conduct of their understanding, and suspect there may be more, and may perhaps serve to excite others to enquire farther into it than the Author hath done.'

Not only is the treatise irregular and incomplete, as a whole, but some of the individual sentences have never been hewn into shape. Locke's customary style, like that of most authors of his time, is much less finished and correct than what we should expect from any writer of the present day, but we can hardly suppose that even he, on revision, would have allowed many of the sentences in this treatise to go into print without some attempt to remodel them. Another defect is the large amount of repetition. These drawbacks, however, are of comparatively little importance, as the meaning is almost always clear, and the terse brevity of the book as a whole, as well as the many racy passages in which it abounds, offer ample amends to the reader for the tediousness of some few sections.

No one acquainted with Bacon's writings can read this treatise, without perceiving Locke's obligations to the first book of the Novum Organum. This fact is the more remarkable, as, with one or two exceptions (See Essay, Bk. II, Ch. 12, § 1, Bk. IV, Ch. 17, § 4, and my introduction to the Novum Organum, § 14, ad init.), there are no specific traces of Bacon's influence in the Essay. It might, however, be justly said that Locke's whole mode of treating philosophical questions is thoroughly imbued with the spirit of the Baconian method.

What is specially remarkable in the mode of handling logical questions in this treatise is the emphasis laid on what may be called the moral causes of fallacious reasoning : prejudice, haste, mental indolence, over-regard for authority, love of antiquity or novelty, self-sufficiency, despondency, and the various other conditions of mind which are quite as effective in barring the way to truth as any sophisms, however skilful, which others may attempt to impose upon us.

The relation of the treatise on the Conduct of the Understanding to the Essay is that of a sort of practical appendix. The one book enquires into the constitution and history of the Human Mind, the other attempts to suggest rules and cautions for guiding or controlling its operations in the search for knowledge. Locke's design, like Bacon's, was to supplement and enlarge the logic of the schools by the addition of practical precepts and warnings, which should be instrumental in leading to the discovery of truth rather than in helping to secure victory in disputation. The more special object of Bacon's method, however, was to overcome the subtlety of nature, and extort from it some account of its secrets; while the scattered hints contained in this treatise of Locke have for their object rather to produce a vigorous understanding, and to suggest improved modes of study and reasoning generally. The treatise abounds in robust common-sense, and, notwithstanding a few flat or tedious passages, it can hardly fail to repay the student for the short time consumed in its perusal.

OF

THE

CONDUCT

OF THE

UNDERSTANDING.

Quid tam temerarium tamque indignum sapientis gravitate atque constantia, quam aut falsum sentire aut quod non satis explorate perceptum sit et cognitum sine ulla dubitatione defendere?—Cic. *De Natura Deorum*, Book I, Chap. I.

SECTION I.

INTRODUCTION.

The last resort a man has recourse to in the conduct of himself is his understanding; for though we distinguish the faculties of the mind, and give the supreme command to the will as to an agent, yet the truth is, the man which is the agent determines himself to this or that voluntary action upon some precedent knowledge, or appearance of knowledge, in the understanding. No man ever sets himself about any thing but upon some view or other which serves him for a reason for what he does: and whatsoever faculties he employs, the understanding, with such light as it has, well or ill informed, constantly leads; and by that light, true or false, all his operative powers are directed. The will itself, how absolute and uncontrollable soever it may be thought, never fails in its obedience to the dictates of the understanding. Temples have their sacred images, and we see what influence they have always had over a great part of mankind. But in truth the ideas and images in men's minds are the invisible powers that constantly govern them, and to these they all universally pay a ready submission. It is therefore of the highest concernment that great care should be taken of the understanding, to conduct it right in the search of knowledge and in the judgments it makes.

The logic now in use has so long possessed the chair, as the only art taught in the schools for the direction of the mind in the study of the arts and sciences, that it would perhaps be thought an affectation of novelty to suspect that rules that have served the learned world these two or three thousand years, and which, without any complaint of defects, the learned have rested in, are not sufficient to guide the understanding. And I should not doubt but this attempt would be censured as vanity or presumption, did not the great Lord Verulam's authority justify it; who, not servilely thinking learning could not be advanced beyond what it was, because for many ages it had not been, did not rest in the lazy approbation and applause of what was, because it was, but enlarged his mind to what might be. In his preface to his *Novum Organum*, concerning logic he pronounces thus: *Qui summas dialecticae partes tribuerunt atque inde fidissima scientiis praesidia comparari putarunt, verissime et optime viderunt intellectum humanum sibi permissum merito suspectum esse debere. Verum infirmior omnino est malo medicina; nec ipsa mali expers. Siquidem dialectica quae recepta est, licet ad civilia et artes quae in sermone et opinione positae sunt rectissime adhibeatur, naturae tamen subtilitatem longo intervallo non attingit; et prensando quod non capit, ad errores potius stabiliendos et quasi figendos quam ad viam veritati aperiendam valuit.*

'They,' says he, 'who attributed so much to logic, perceived very well and truly, that it was not safe to trust the understanding to itself, without the guard of any rules. But the remedy reached not the evil; but became a part of it: for the logic which took place, though it might do well enough in civil affairs and the arts which consisted in talk and opinion, yet comes very far short of subtilty in the real performances of nature, and, catching at what it cannot reach, has served to confirm and establish errors, rather than to open a way to truth.' And therefore a little after he says, ' That it is absolutely necessary that a better and perfecter use and employment of the mind and understanding should be introduced.' *Necessario requiritur ut melior et perfectior mentis et intellectus humani usus et adoperatio introducatur.*

SECTION II.

PARTS.

There is, it is visible, great variety in men's understandings, and their natural constitutions put so wide a difference between some men in this respect, that art and industry would never be able to master; and their very natures seem to want a foundation to raise on it that which other men easily attain unto.—Amongst men of equal education there is great inequality of parts. And the woods of America, as well as the schools of Athens, produce men of several abilities in the same kind. Though this be so, yet I imagine most men come very short of what they might attain unto in their several degrees by a neglect of their understandings. A few rules of logic are thought sufficient in this case for those who pretend to the highest improvement; whereas I think there are a great many natural defects in the understanding capable of amendment, which are overlooked and wholly neglected. And it is easy to perceive that men are guilty of a great many faults in the exercise and improvement of this faculty of the mind, which hinder them in their progress and keep them in ignorance and error all their lives.

Some of them I shall take notice of, and endeavour to point out proper remedies for in the following discourse.

SECTION III.

REASONING.

Besides the want of determined ideas, and of sagacity and exercise in finding out and laying in order intermediate ideas, there are three miscarriages that men are guilty of in reference to their reason, whereby this faculty is hindered in them from that service it might do and was designed for. And he that reflects upon the actions and discourses of mankind, will find their defects in this kind very frequent and very observable.

1. The first is of those who seldom reason at all, but do and think according to the example of others, whether parents, neighbours, ministers, or who else they are pleased to make choice of to have an implicit faith in, for the saving of themselves the pains and trouble of thinking and examining for themselves.

2. The second is of those who put passion in the place of reason, and, being resolved that shall govern their actions and arguments, neither use their own nor hearken to other people's reason, any farther than it suits their humour, interest, or party; and these one may observe commonly content themselves with words which have no distinct ideas to them, though, in other matters, that they come with an unbiassed indifferency to, they want not abilities to talk and hear reason, where they have no secret inclination that hinders them from being tractable to it.

3. The third sort is of those who readily and sincerely

follow reason, but, for want of having that which one may call *large, sound, round-about sense,* have not a full view of all that relates to the question and may be of moment to decide it. We are all short sighted, and very often see but one side of a matter; our views are not extended to all that has a connection with it. From this defect I think no man is free. We see but in part, and we know but in part, and therefore it is no wonder we conclude not right from our partial views. This might instruct the proudest esteemer of his own parts, how useful it is to talk and consult with others, even such as come short of him in capacity, quickness and penetration : for since no one sees all, and we generally have different prospects of the same thing, according to our different, as I may say, positions to it, it is not incongruous to think nor beneath any man to try, whether another may not have notions of things which have escaped him, and which his reason would make use of if they came into his mind. The faculty of reasoning seldom or never deceives those who trust to it; its consequences from what it builds on are evident and certain, but that which it oftenest, if not only, misleads us in is that the principles from which we conclude, the grounds upon which we bottom our reasoning, are but a part, something is left out which should go into the reckoning to make it just and exact. Here we may imagine a vast and almost infinite advantage that angels and separate spirits may have over us; who, in their several degrees of elevation above us, may be endowed with more comprehensive faculties, and some of them perhaps have perfect and exact views of all finite beings that come under their consideration, can, as it were, in the twinkling of an eye, collect together all their scattered and almost boundless relations. A mind so furnished, what reason has it to acquiesce in the certainty of its conclusions!

In this we may see the reason why some men of study and thought, that reason right and are lovers of truth, do make no great advances in their discoveries of it. Error and truth are uncertainly blended in their minds; their decisions are lame and defective, and they are very often mistaken in their judgments: the reason whereof is, they converse but with one sort of men, they read but one sort of books, they will not come in the hearing but of one sort of notions; the truth is, they canton out to themselves a little Goshen in the intellectual world, where light shines, and, as they conclude, day blesses them; but the rest of that vast *Expansum* they give up to night and darkness, and so avoid coming near it. They have a pretty traffick with known correspondents in some little creek; within that they confine themselves, and are dexterous managers enough of the wares and products of that corner with which they content themselves, but will not venture out into the great ocean of knowledge, to survey the riches that nature hath stored other parts with, no less genuine, no less solid, no less useful, than what has fallen to their lot in the admired plenty and sufficiency of their own little spot, which to them contains whatsoever is good in the universe. Those who live thus mued up within their own contracted territories, and will not look abroad beyond the boundaries that chance, conceit, or laziness has set to their enquiries, but live separate from the notions, discourses and attainments of the rest of mankind, may not amiss be represented by the inhabitants of the Marian islands; who, being separated by a large tract of sea from all communion with the habitable parts of the earth, thought themselves the only people of

the world. And though the straitness of the conveniences
of life amongst them had never reached so far as to the
use of fire, till the Spaniards, not many years since, in
their voyages from Acapulco to Manilia brought it
amongst them; yet in the want and ignorance of almost
all things, they looked upon themselves, even after that
the Spaniards had brought amongst them the notice of
variety of nations abounding in sciences, arts and conveniences of life, of which they knew nothing, they looked
upon themselves, I say, as the happiest and wisest people
of the universe. But for all that, no body, I think, will
imagine them deep naturalists, or solid metaphysicians;
no body will deem the quickest sighted amongst them to
have very enlarged views in ethics or politics, nor can any
one allow the most capable amongst them to be advanced so
far in his understanding as to have any other knowledge
but of the few little things of his and the neighbouring
islands within his commerce, but far enough from that
comprehensive enlargement of mind which adorns a soul
devoted to truth, assisted with letters, and a free consideration of the several views and sentiments of thinking
men of all sides. Let not men therefore that would have
a sight of, what every one pretends to be desirous to have
a sight of, truth in its full extent, narrow and blind their
own prospect. Let not men think there is no truth but
in the sciences that they study, or the books that they
read. To prejudge other men's notions before we have
looked into them is not to shew their darkness, but to put
out our own eyes. *Try all things, hold fast that which is
good*, is a divine rule coming from the Father of light and
truth; and it is hard to know what other way men can
come at truth, to lay hold of it, if they do not dig and
search for it as for gold and hid treasure; but he that

does so must have much earth and rubbish before he gets
the pure metal; sand, and pebbles, and dross usually lie
blended with it, but the gold is nevertheless gold, and will
enrich the man that employs his pains to seek and separate it. Neither is there any danger he should be deceived
by the mixture. Every man carries about him a touchstone, if he will make use of it, to distinguish substantial
gold from superficial glitterings, truth from appearances.
And indeed the use and benefit of this touchstone, which
is natural reason, is spoiled and lost only by assumed
prejudices, overweening presumption, and narrowing our
minds. The want of exercising it in the full extent of
things intelligible, is that which weakens and extinguishes
this noble faculty in us. Trace it, and see whether it be
not so. The day labourer in a country village has commonly but a small pittance of knowledge, because his
ideas and notions have been confined to the narrow
bounds of a poor conversation and employment; the low
mechanic of a country town does somewhat outdo him;
porters and cobblers of great cities surpass them. A
country gentleman, who, leaving Latin and Learning in
the university, removes thence to his mansion house, and
associates with neighbours of the same strain, who relish
nothing but hunting and a bottle; with those alone he
spends his time, with those alone he converses, and
can away with no company whose discourse goes beyond what claret and dissoluteness inspire. Such a
patriot, formed in this·happy way of improvement, cannot fail, as we see, to give notable decisions upon the
bench at quarter sessions, and eminent proofs of his skill
in politics, when the strength of his purse and party have
advanced him to a more conspicuous station. To such a
one truly an ordinary coffee-house gleaner of the city is

an errant statesman, and as much superior to, as a man conversant about Whitehall and the court is to an ordinary shopkeeper. To carry this a little farther. Here is one muffled up in the zeal and infallibility of his own sect, and will not touch a book or enter into debate with a person that will question any of those things which to him are sacred. Another surveys our differences in religion with an equitable and fair indifference, and so finds probably that none of them are in every thing unexceptionable. These divisions and systems were made by men, and carry the mark of fallible on them; and in those whom he differs from, and, till he opened his eyes, had a general prejudice against, he meets with more to be said for a great many things than before he was aware of, or could have imagined. Which of these two now is most likely to judge right in our religious controversies, and to be most stored with truth, the mark all pretend to aim at? All these men that I have instanced in, thus unequally furnished with truth and advanced in knowledge, I suppose of equal natural parts; all the odds between them has been the different scope that has been given to their understandings to range in, for the gathering up of information, and furnishing their heads with ideas, notions and observations, whereon to employ their minds and form their understandings.

It will possibly be objected, who is sufficient for all this? I answer, more than can be imagined. Every one knows what his proper business is, and what, according to the character he makes of himself, the world may justly expect of him; and to answer that, he will find he will have time and opportunity enough to furnish himself, if he will not deprive himself by a narrowness of spirit of those helps that are at hand. I do not say to be a good geographer that a man should visit every mountain, river, promontory and creek upon the face of the earth, view the buildings, and survey the land every where, as if he were going to make a purchase.   But yet every one must allow that he shall know a country better that makes often sallies into it, and traverses it up and down, than he that like a mill horse goes still round in the same track, or keeps within the narrow bounds of a field or two that delight him.   He that will enquire out the best books in every science, and inform himself of the most material authors of the several sects of philosophy and religion, will not find it an infinite work to acquaint himself with the sentiments of mankind concerning the most weighty and comprehensive subjects.   Let him exercise the freedom of his reason and understanding in such a latitude as this, and his mind will be strengthened, his capacity enlarged, his faculties improved ; and the light, which the remote and scattered parts of truth will give to one another, will so assist his judgment, that he will seldom be widely out, or miss giving proof of a clear head and a comprehensive knowledge.   At least, this is the only way I know to give the understanding its due improvement to the full extent of its capacity, and to distinguish the two most different things I know in the world, a logical chicaner from a man of reason.   Only, he that would thus give the mind its flight, and send abroad his enquiries into all parts after truth, must be sure to settle in his head determined ideas of all that he employs his thoughts about, and never fail to judge himself, and judge unbiassedly of all that he receives from others, either in their writings or discourses.   Reverence or prejudice must not be suffered to give beauty or deformity to any of their opinions.

SECTION IV.

PRACTICE AND HABITS.

We are born with faculties and powers capable almost of any thing, such at least as would carry us farther than can easily be imagined: but it is only the exercise of those powers which gives us ability and skill in any thing, and leads us towards perfection.

A middle-aged ploughman will scarce ever be brought to the carriage and language of a gentleman, though his body be as well proportioned, and his joints as supple, and his natural parts not any way inferior. The legs of a dancing master and the fingers of a musician fall as it were naturally, without thought or pains, into regular and admirable motions. Bid them change their parts, and they will in vain endeavour to produce like motions in the members not used to them, and it will require length of time and long practice to attain but some degrees of a like ability. What incredible and astonishing actions do we find rope dancers and tumblers bring their bodies to; not but that sundry in almost all manual arts are as wonderful; but I name those which the world takes notice of for such, because on that very account they give money to see them. All these admired motions beyond the reach, and almost the conception, of unpractised spectators are nothing but the mere effects of use and industry in men, whose bodies have nothing peculiar in them from those of the amazed lookers on.

As it is in the body, so it is in the mind; practice makes it what it is, and most even of those excellences which are looked on as natural endowments will be found, when examined into more narrowly, to be the product of exercise, and to be raised to that pitch only by repeated actions. Some men are remarked for pleasantness in raillery; others for apologues and apposite diverting stories. This is apt to be taken for the effect of pure nature, and that the rather, because it is not got by rules, and those who excel in either of them never purposely set themselves to the study of it as an art to be learnt. But yet it is true that at first some lucky hit, which took with some body and gained him commendation, encouraged him to try again, inclined his thoughts and endeavours that way, till at last he insensibly got a facility in it without perceiving how; and that is attributed wholly to nature which was much more the effect of use and practice. I do not deny that natural disposition may often give the first rise to it; but that never carries a man far without use and exercise, and it is practice alone that brings the powers of the mind as well as those of the body to their perfection. Many a good poetic vein is buried under a trade, and never produces any thing for want of improvement. We see the ways of discourse and reasoning are very different, even concerning the same matter, at court and in the university. And he that will go but from Westminster-hall to the Exchange, will find a different genius and turn in their ways of talking, and yet one cannot think that all whose lot fell in the city were born with different parts from those who were bred at the university or inns of court.

To what purpose all this, but to shew that the difference, so observable in men's understandings and parts, does not arise so much from their natural faculties as acquired habits. He would be laughed at that should go about to make a fine dancer out of a country hedger, at past fifty. And he will not have much better success, who shall endeavour at that age to make a man reason well, or speak handsomely, who has never been used to it, though you should lay before him a collection of all the best precepts of logic or oratory. No body is made any thing by hearing of rules, or laying them up in his memory; practice must settle the habit of doing without reflecting on the rule, and you may as well hope to make a good painter or musician extempore by a lecture and instruction in the arts of music and painting, as a coherent thinker or strict reasoner by a set of rules, shewing him wherein right reasoning consists.

This being so, that defects and weakness in men's understandings, as well as other faculties, come from want of a right use of their own minds, I am apt to think the fault is generally mislaid upon nature, and there is often a complaint of want of parts, when the fault lies in want of a due improvement of them. We see men frequently dexterous and sharp enough in making a bargain, who, if you reason with them about matters of religion, appear perfectly stupid.

SECTION V.

IDEAS.

I will not here, in what relates to the right conduct and improvement of the understanding, repeat again the getting clear and determined ideas, and the employing our thoughts rather about them than about sounds put for them, nor of settling the signification of words which we use with ourselves in the search of truth or with others in discoursing about it. Those hindrances of our understandings in the pursuit of knowledge, I have sufficiently enlarged upon in another place; so that nothing more needs here to be said of those matters.

SECTION VI.

PRINCIPLES.

There is another fault that stops or misleads men in their knowledge, which I have also spoken something of, but yet is necessary to mention here again, that we may examine it to the bottom and see the root it springs from, and that is a custom of taking up with principles that are not self-evident and very often not so much as true. It is not unusual to see men rest their opinions upon foundations that have no more certainty and solidity than the propositions built on them and embraced for their sake. Such foundations are these and the like, namely: the founders or leaders of my party are good men, and therefore their tenets are true; it is the opinion of a sect that is erroneous, therefore it is false; it hath been long received in the world, therefore it is true; or it is new, and therefore false.

These, and many the like, which are by no means the measures of truth and falsehood, the generality of men make the standards by which they accustom their understanding to judge. And thus they falling into a habit of determining truth and falsehood by such wrong measures, it is no wonder they should embrace error for certainty, and be very positive in things they have no ground for.

There is not any who pretends to the least reason, but, when any of these his false maxims are brought to the test, must acknowledge them to be fallible, and such as he will not allow in those that differ from him; and yet, after he is convinced of this, you shall see him go on in the use of them, and the very next occasion that offers argue again upon the same grounds. Would one not be ready to think that men are willing to impose upon themselves and mislead their own understandings, who conduct them by such wrong measures, even after they see they cannot be relied on? But yet they will not appear so blameable as may be thought at first sight; for I think there are a great many that argue thus in earnest, and do it not to impose on themselves or others. They are persuaded of what they say, and think there is weight in it, though in a like case they have been convinced there is none; but men would be intolerable to themselves, and contemptible to others, if they should embrace opinions without any ground, and hold what they could give no manner of reason for. True or false, solid or sandy, the mind must have some foundation to rest itself upon, and, as I have remarked in another place, it no sooner entertains any proposition, but it frequently hastens to some hypothesis to bottom it on; till then it is unquiet and unsettled. So much do our own very tempers dispose us to a right use of our understandings, if we would follow as we should the inclinations of our nature.

In some matters of concernment, especially those of religion, men are not permitted to be always wavering and uncertain, they must embrace and profess some tenets or other; and it would be a shame, nay, a contradiction too heavy for any one's mind to lie constantly under, for him to pretend seriously to be persuaded of the truth of any religion, and yet not to be able to give any reason of his belief, or to say any thing for his preference of this to any other opinion. And therefore they must make use of some principles or other, and those can be no other than such as they have and can manage; and to say they are not in earnest persuaded by them, and do not rest upon those they make use of, is contrary to experience, and to allege that they are not misled when we complain they are.

If this be so, it will be urged, why then do they not rather make use of sure and unquestionable principles, than rest on such grounds as may deceive them, and will, as is visible, serve to support error as well as truth?

To this I answer, the reason why they do not make use of better and surer principles, is because they cannot; but this inability proceeds not from want of natural parts (for those few whose case that is are to be excused) but for want of use and exercise. Few men are from their youth accustomed to strict reasoning, and to trace the dependence of any truth in a long train of consequences to its remote principles, and to observe its connection; and he that by frequent practice has not been used to this employment of his understanding, it is no more wonder that he should not, when he is grown into years, be able to bring his mind to it, than that he should not be on a sudden able to grave or design, dance on the ropes, or write a good hand, who has never practised either of them.

Nay, the most of men are so wholly strangers to this, that they do not so much as perceive their want of it. They dispatch the ordinary business of their callings by rote, as we say, as they have learnt it, and, if at any time they miss success, they impute it to any thing rather than want of thought or skill; that they conclude (because they know no better) they have in perfection. Or if there be any subject that interest or fancy has recommended to their thoughts, their reasoning about it is still after their own fashion; be it better or worse, it serves their turns, and is the best they are acquainted with: and therefore when they are led by it into mistakes, and their business succeeds accordingly, they impute it to any cross

accident, or default of others, rather than to their own
want of understanding ; that is what no body discovers
or complains of in himself.   Whatsoever made his business to miscarry, it was not want of right thought and
judgment in himself : he sees no such defect in himself,
but is satisfied that he carries on his designs well enough
by his own reasoning, or at least should have done, had
it not been for unlucky traverses not in his power.   Thus
being content with this short and very imperfect use of
his understanding, he never troubles himself to seek out
methods of improving his mind, and lives all his life
without any notion of close reasoning in a continued
connection of a long train of consequences from sure
foundations, such as is requisite for the making out and
clearing most of the speculative truths most men own
to believe and are most concerned in.   Not to mention
here what I shall have occasion to insist on by and by
more fully, namely, that in many cases it is not one
series of consequences will serve the turn, but many
different and opposite deductions must be examined and
laid together, before a man can come to make a right
judgment of the point in question.   What then can be
expected from men that neither see the want of any such
kind of reasoning as this, nor, if they do, know they how
to set about it, or could perform it ? You may as well
set a countryman who scarce knows the figures, and
never cast up a sum of three particulars, to state a merchant's long account, and find the true balance of it.

What then should be done in the case ? I answer, we
should always remember what I said above, that the
faculties of our souls are improved and made useful to
us just after the same manner as our bodies are.   Would
you have a man write or paint, dance or fence well, or

perform any other manual operation dexterously and with
ease, let him have ever so much vigour and activity, suppleness and address naturally, yet no body expects this
from him unless he has been used to it, and has employed time and pains in fashioning and forming his
hand or outward parts to these motions. Just so it is in
the mind; would you have a man reason well, you must
use him to it betimes, exercise his mind in observing the
connection of ideas and following them in train. Nothing
does this better than mathematics, which therefore I think
should be taught all those who have the time and opportunity, not so much to make them mathematicians as to
make them reasonable creatures; for though we all call
ourselves so, because we are born to it if we please, yet
we may truly say nature gives us but the seeds of it; we
are born to be, if we please, rational creatures, but it is
use and exercise only that makes us so, and we are indeed so no farther than industry and application has
carried us. And therefore, in ways of reasoning which
men have not been used to, he that will observe the
conclusions they take up must be satisfied they are not
†at† all rational.

This has been the less taken notice of, because every
one, in his private affairs, uses some sort of reasoning or
other, enough to denominate him reasonable. But the
mistake is, that he that is found reasonable in one thing
is concluded to be so in all, and to think or say otherwise
is thought so unjust an affront, and so senseless a cen-
sure, that no body ventures to do it. It looks like the
degradation of a man below the dignity of his nature. It
is true that he that reasons well in any one thing has a
mind naturally capable of reasoning well in others, and
to the same degree of strength and clearness, and pos-

sibly much greater, had his understanding been so employed. But it is as true that he, who can reason well to day about one sort of matters, cannot at all reason to day about others, though perhaps a year hence he may. But wherever a man's rational faculty fails him, and will not serve him to reason, there we cannot say he is rational, how capable soever he may be by time and exercise to become so.

Try in men of low and mean education, who have never elevated their thoughts above the spade and the plough, nor looked beyond the ordinary drudgery of a day labourer. Take the thoughts of such an one, used for many years to one track, out of that narrow compass he has been all his life confined to, you will find him no more capable of reasoning than almost a perfect natural. Some one or two rules, on which their conclusions immediately depend, you will find in most men have governed all their thoughts; these, true or false, have been the maxims they have been guided by: take these from them, and they are perfectly at a loss, their compass and pole star then are gone, and their understanding is perfectly at a nonplus, and therefore they either immediately return to their old maxims again as the foundations of all truth to them, notwithstanding all that can be said to shew their weakness, or, if they give them up to their reasons, they with them give up all truth and further enquiry, and think there is no such thing as certainty. For if you would enlarge their thoughts, and settle them upon more remote and surer principles, they either cannot easily apprehend them, or, if they can, know not what use to make of them ; for long deductions from remote principles is what they have not been used to, and cannot manage.

What then, can grown men never be improved or enlarged in their understandings? I say not so, but this I think I may say, that it will not be done without industry and application, which will require more time and pains than grown men, settled in their course of life, will allow to it, and therefore very seldom is done. And this very capacity of attaining it by use and exercise only brings us back to that which I laid down before, that it is only practice that improves our minds as well as bodies, and we must expect nothing from our understandings any farther than they are perfected by habits.

The Americans are not all born with worse understandings than the Europeans, though we see none of them have such reaches in the arts and sciences. And among the children of a poor countryman, the lucky chance of education and getting into the world gives one infinitely the superiority in parts over the rest, who, continuing at home, had continued also just of the same size with his brethren.

He that has to do with young scholars, especially in mathematics, may perceive how their minds open by degrees, and how it is exercise alone that opens them. Sometimes they will stick a long time at a part of a demonstration, not for want of will and application, but really for want of perceiving the connection of two ideas that, to one whose understanding is more exercised, is as visible as any thing can be. The same would be with a grown man beginning to study mathematics; the understanding, for want of use, often sticks in very plain way, and he himself that is so puzzled, when he comes to see the connection, wonders what it was he stuck at in a case so plain.

SECTION VII.

MATHEMATICS.

I have mentioned mathematics as a way to settle in the mind a habit of reasoning closely and in train ; not that I think it necessary that all men should be deep mathematicians, but that having got the way of reasoning, which that study necessarily brings the mind to, they might be able to transfer it to other parts of knowledge as they shall have occasion. For, in all sorts of reasoning, every single argument should be managed as a mathematical demonstration, the connection and dependence of ideas should be followed till the mind is brought to the source on which it bottoms and observes the coherence all along, though, in proofs of probability, one such train is not enough to settle the judgment as in demonstrative knowledge.

Where a truth is made out by one demonstration, there needs no farther enquiry, but in probabilities where there wants demonstration to establish the truth beyond doubt, there it is not enough to trace one argument to its source, and observe its strength and weakness, but all the arguments, after having been so examined on both sides, must be laid in balance one against another, and upon the whole the understanding determine its assent.

This is a way of reasoning the understanding should be accustomed to, which is so different from what the illiterate are used to, that even learned men oftentimes seem to have very little or no notion of it. Nor is it to be wondered, since the way of disputing in the schools leads them quite away from it, by insisting on one topical argument, by the success of which the truth or falsehood of the question is to be determined and victory adjudged to the opponent or defendant; which is all one as if one should balance an account by one sum charged and discharged, when there are an hundred others to be taken into consideration.

This therefore it would be well if men's minds were accustomed to, and that early, that they might not erect their opinions upon one single view, when so many other are requisite to make up the account, and must come into the reckoning before a man can form a right judgment. This would enlarge their minds, and give a due freedom to their understandings, that they might not be led into error by presumption, laziness or precipitancy; for I think no body can approve such a conduct of the understanding as should mislead it from truth, though it be ever so much in fashion to make use of it.

To this perhaps it will be objected, that to manage the understanding, as I propose, would require every man to be a scholar, and to be furnished with all the materials of knowledge, and exercised in all the ways of reasoning. To which I answer, that it is a shame for those that have time and the means to attain knowledge, to want any helps or assistance for the improvement of their understandings that are to be got, and to such I would be thought here chiefly to speak. Those methinks, who by the industry and parts of their ancestors have been set free from a constant drudgery to their backs and their bellies, should bestow some of their spare time on their heads, and open their minds by some trials and essays in all the sorts and matters of reasoning. I have before mentioned mathematics, wherein algebra gives new helps and views to the understanding. If I propose these, it is not, as I said, to make every man a thorough mathematician, or a deep algebraist; but yet I think the study of them is of infinite use even to grown men.

First by experimentally convincing them that, to make any one reason well, it is not enough to have parts where-with he is satisfied and that serve him well enough in his ordinary course. A man in those studies will see that, however good he may think his understanding, yet in many things, and those very visible, it may fail him. This would take off that presumption that most men have of themselves in this part; and they would not be so apt to think their minds wanted no helps to enlarge them, that there could be nothing added to the acuteness and penetration of their understandings.

Secondly, the study of mathematics would shew them the necessity there is, in reasoning, to separate all the distinct ideas, and see the habitudes that all those concerned in the present enquiry have to one another, and to lay by those which relate not to the proposition in hand and wholly to leave them out of the reckoning. This is that which in other subjects, besides quantity, is what is absolutely requisite to just reasoning, though in them it is not so easily observed nor so carefully practised. In those parts of knowledge where it is thought demonstration has nothing to do, men reason as it were in the lump: and, if, upon a summary and confused view or upon a partial consideration, they can raise the appearance of a probability, they usually rest content; especially if it be in a dispute where every little straw is laid hold on, and every thing that can but be drawn in any way to give colour to the argument is advanced with ostentation. But that mind is not in a posture to find the truth, that does not distinctly take all the parts asunder, and, omitting what is not at all to the point, draw a conclusion from the result of all the

particulars which any way influence it.   There is another
no less useful habit to be got by an application to mathematical demonstrations, and that is, of using the mind to
a long train of consequences; but, having mentioned that
already, I shall not again here repeat it.

As to men whose fortunes and time is narrower, what
may suffice them is not of that vast extent as may be
imagined, and so comes not within the objection.

No body is under an obligation to know every thing.
Knowledge and science in general is the business only
of those who are at ease and leisure.   Those who have
particular callings ought to understand them ; and it is no
unreasonable proposal, nor impossible to be compassed,
that they should think and reason right about what is their
daily employment. This one cannot think them incapable
of, without levelling them with the brutes, and charging
them with a stupidity below the rank of rational creatures.

SECTION VIII.

RELIGION.

Besides his particular calling for the support of this
life, every one has a concern in a future life, which he is
bound to look after.   This engages his thoughts in
religion; and here it mightily lies upon him to understand
and reason right.   Men therefore cannot be excused from
understanding the words, and framing the general notions,
relating to religion right.   The one day of seven, besides
other days of rest, allows in the christian world time
enough for this (had they no other idle hours), if they
would but make use of these vacancies from their daily
labour, and apply themselves to an improvement of

knowledge, with as much diligence as they often do to a great many other things that are useless, and had but those that would enter them according to their several capacities in a right way to this knowledge. The original make of their minds is like that of other men, and they would be found not to want understanding fit to receive the knowledge of religion, if they were a little encouraged and helped in it as they should be. For there are instances of very mean people, who have raised their minds to a great sense and understanding of religion. And though these have not been so frequent as could be wished, yet they are enough to clear that condition of life from a necessity of gross ignorance, and to shew that more might be brought to be rational creatures and christians (for they can hardly be thought really to be so, who, wearing the name, know not so much as the very principles of that religion) if due care were taken of them. For, if I mistake not, the peasantry lately in France (a rank of people under a much heavier pressure of want and poverty than the day labourers in England) of the reformed religion understood it much better, and could say more for it, than those of a higher condition among us.

But if it shall be concluded that the meaner sort of people must give themselves up to a brutish stupidity in the things of their nearest concernment, which I see no reason for, this excuses not those of a freer fortune and education, if they neglect their understandings, and take no care to employ them as they ought and set them right in the knowledge of those things for which principally they were given them. At least those whose plentiful fortunes allow them the opportunities and helps of improvements are not so few, but that it might be hoped great advancements might be made in knowledge of all kinds, especially in that of the greatest concern and largest views, if men would make a right use of their faculties and study their own understandings.

SECTION IX.

IDEAS.

Outward corporeal objects that constantly importune our senses, and captivate our appetites, fail not to fill our heads with lively and lasting ideas of that kind. Here the mind needs not be set upon getting greater store; they offer themselves fast enough, and are usually entertained in such plenty and lodged so carefully, that the mind wants room or attention for others that it has more use and need of. To fit the understanding therefore for such reasoning as I have been above speaking of, care should be taken to fill it with moral and more abstract ideas; for these not offering themselves to the senses, but being to be framed to the understanding, people are generally so neglectful of a faculty they are apt to think wants nothing, that I fear most men's minds are more unfurnished with such ideas than is imagined. They often use the words, and how can they be suspected to want the ideas? What I have said in the third book of my essay, will excuse me from any other answer to this question. But to convince people of what moment it is to their understandings to be furnished with such abstract ideas steady and settled in them, give me leave to ask how any one shall be able to know whether he be obliged to be just, if he has not established ideas in his mind of obligation and of justice, since knowledge consists in nothing but the perceived agreement or disagreement of those ideas ; and so of all others the like which concern our lives and manners. And if men do find a difficulty to see the agreement or disagreement of two angles which lie before their eyes, unalterable in a diagram, how utterly impossible will it be to perceive it in ideas that have no other sensible objects to represent them to the mind but sounds with which they have no manner of conformity, and therefore had need to be clearly settled in the mind themselves, if we would make any clear judgment about them. This therefore is one of the first things the mind should be employed about in the right conduct of the understanding, without which it is impossible it should be capable of reasoning right about those matters. But in these and all other ideas, care must be taken that they harbour no inconsistences, and that they have a real existence where real existence is supposed, and are not mere chimeras with a supposed existence.

SECTION X.

PREJUDICE.

Every one is forward to complain of the prejudices that mislead other men or parties, as if he were free, and had none of his own. This being objected on all sides, it is agreed that it is a fault and an hindrance to knowledge. What now is the cure? No other but this, that every man should let alone others' prejudices and examine his own. No body is convinced of his by the accusation of another ; he recriminates by the same rule, and is clear. The only way to remove this great cause of ignorance and error out of the world is for every one impartially to examine himself. If others will not deal fairly with their own minds, does that make my errors truths, or ought it to make me in love with them and willing to impose on myself? If others love cataracts on their eyes, should that hinder me from couching of mine as soon as I could? Every one declares against blindness, and yet who almost is not fond of that which dims his sight, and keeps the clear light out of his mind, which should lead him into truth and knowledge? False or doubtful positions, relied upon as unquestionable maxims, keep those in the dark from truth, who build on them. Such are usually the prejudices imbibed from education, party, reverence, fashion, interest, &c. This is the mote which every one sees in his brother's eye, but never regards the beam in his own. For who is there almost that is ever brought fairly to examine his own principles, and see whether they are such as will bear the trial? but yet this should be one of the first things every one should set about, and be scrupulous in, who would rightly conduct his understanding in the search of truth and knowledge.

To those who are willing to get rid of this great hindrance of knowledge—for to such only I write—to those who would shake off this great and dangerous impostor prejudice, who dresses up falsehood in the likeness of truth, and so dexterously hoodwinks men's minds as to keep them in the dark with a belief that they are more in the light than any that do not see with their eyes, I shall offer this one mark whereby prejudice may be known. He that is strongly of any opinion, must suppose (unless he be self-condemned) that his persuasion is built upon good grounds, and that his assent is no greater than what the evidence of the truth he holds forces him to, and that they are arguments and not inclination or fancy that make him so confident and positive in his tenets.   Now if, after all his profession, he cannot bear any opposition to his opinion, if he cannot so much as give a patient hearing, much less examine and weigh the arguments on the other side, does he not plainly confess it is prejudice governs him? And it is not the evidence of truth, but some lazy anticipation, some beloved presumption that he desires to rest undisturbed in.   For if what he holds be, as he gives out, well fenced with evidence, and he sees it to be true, what need he fear to put it to the proof?   If his opinion be settled upon a firm foundation, if the arguments that support it and have obtained his assent be clear, good, and convincing, why should he be shy to have it tried whether they be proof or not?   He whose assent goes beyond his evidence owes this excess of his adherence only to prejudice, and does, in effect, own it, when he refuses to hear what is offered against it; declaring thereby that it is not evidence he seeks, but the quiet enjoyment of the opinion he is fond of, with a forward condemnation of all that may stand in opposition to it, unheard and unexamined; which, what is it but prejudice? *Qui aequum statuerit parte inauditâ alterâ, etiam si aequum statuerit, haud aequus fuerit.*   He that would acquit himself in this case as a lover of truth, not giving way to any preoccupation or bias that may mislead him, must do two things that are not very common nor very easy.

SECTION XI.

INDIFFERENCY.

First, he must not be in love with any opinion, or wish it to be true, till he knows it to be so, and then he will not need to wish it: for nothing that is false can deserve our good wishes, nor a desire that it should have the place and force of truth; and yet nothing is more frequent than this. Men are fond of certain tenets upon no other evidence but respect and custom, and think they must maintain them, or all is gone, though they have never examined the ground they stand on, nor have ever made them out to themselves, or can make them out to others. We should contend earnestly for the truth, but we should first be sure that it is truth, or else we fight against God, who is the God of truth, and do the work of the devil, who is the father and propagator of lies; and our zeal, though ever so warm, will not excuse us; for this is plainly prejudice.

SECTION XII.

EXAMINE.

Secondly, he must do that which he will find himself very averse to, as judging the thing unnecessary or himself incapable of doing it. He must try whether his principles be certainly true or not, and how far he may safely rely upon them. This, whether fewer have the heart or the skill to do, I shall not determine; but this I am sure, this is that which every one ought to do, who professes to love truth and would not impose upon himself; which is a surer way to be made a fool of than by being exposed to the sophistry of others. The disposition to put any cheat upon ourselves works constantly, and we are pleased with it, but are impatient of being bantered or misled by others. The inability I here speak of is not any natural defect that makes men incapable of examining their own principles. To such, rules of conducting their understandings are useless, and that is the case of very few. The great number is of those whom the ill habit of never exerting their thoughts has disabled : the powers of their minds are starved by disuse, and have lost that reach and strength which nature fitted them to receive from exercise. Those who are in a condition to learn the first rules of plain arithmetic, and could be brought to cast up an ordinary sum, are capable of this, if they had but accustomed their minds to reasoning : but they that have wholly neglected the exercise of their understandings in this way will be very far at first from being able to do it, and as unfit for it as one unpractised in figures to cast up a shopbook, and perhaps think it as strange to be set about it. And yet it must nevertheless be confessed to be a wrong use of our understandings to build our tenets (in things where we are concerned to hold the truth) upon principles that may lead us into error. We take our principles at haphazard upon trust, and without ever having examined them, and then believe a whole system, upon a presumption that they are true and solid; and what is all this but childish, shameful, senseless credulity ?

In these two things, namely, an equal indifferency for all truth, I mean the receiving it in the love of it as truth, but not loving it for any other reason before we know it to be true, and in the examination of our principles, and not receiving any for such nor building on them till we are fully convinced, as rational creatures, of their solidity, truth, and certainty, consists that freedom of the understanding which is necessary to a rational creature, and without which it is not truly an understanding. It is conceit, fancy, extravagance, any thing rather than understanding, if it must be under the constraint of receiving and holding opinions by the authority of any thing but their own, not fancied, but perceived, evidence. This was rightly called imposition, and is of all other the worst and most dangerous sort of it. For we impose upon ourselves, which is the strongest imposition of all others; and we impose upon ourselves in that part which ought with the greatest care to be kept free from all imposition. The world is apt to cast great blame on those who have an indifferency for opinions, especially in religion. I fear this is the foundation of great error and worse consequences. To be indifferent which of two opinions is true, is the right temper of the mind that preserves it from being imposed on, and disposes it to examine with that indifferency, till it has done its best to find the truth, and this is the only direct and safe way to it. But to be indifferent whether we embrace falsehood or truth or no, is the great road to error. Those who are not indifferent which opinion is true are guilty of this; they suppose, without examining, that what they hold is true, and then think they ought to be zealous for it. Those, it is plain by their warmth and eagerness, are not indifferent for their own opinions, but methinks are very indifferent whether they be true or false, since they cannot endure to have any doubts raised or objections made against them; and it is visible they never have made any themselves, and so, never having examined them, know not nor are concerned, as they should be, to know whether they be true or false.

These are the common and most general miscarriages which I think men should avoid or rectify in a right conduct of their understandings, and should be particularly taken care of in education. The business whereof in respect of knowledge is not, as I think, to perfect a learner in all or any one of the sciences, but to give his mind that freedom, that disposition, and those habits that may enable him to attain any part of knowledge he shall apply himself to, or stand in need of, in the future course of his life.

This and this only is well principling, and not the instilling a reverence and veneration for certain dogmas under the specious title of principles, which are often so remote from that truth and evidence which belongs to principles that they ought to be rejected as false and erroneous, and is often the cause, to men so educated, when they come abroad into the world, and find they cannot maintain the principles so taken up and rested in, to cast off all principles and turn perfect sceptics, regardless of knowledge and virtue.

There are several weaknesses and defects in the understanding, either from the natural temper of the mind or ill habits taken up, which hinder it in its progress to knowledge. Of these there are as many possibly to be found, if the mind were thoroughly studied, as there are diseases of the body, each whereof clogs and disables the understanding to some degree, and therefore deserves to be looked after and cured. I shall set down some few to excite men, especially those who make knowledge their business, to look into themselves, and observe whether they do not indulge some weakness, allow some miscarriages in the management of their intellectual faculty, which is prejudicial to them in the search of truth.

SECTION XIII.

OBSERVATION.

Particular matters of fact are the undoubted foundations on which our civil and natural knowledge is built; the benefit the understanding makes of them is to draw from them conclusions, which may be as standing rules of knowledge, and consequently of practice. The mind often makes not that benefit it should of the information it receives from the accounts of civil or natural historians, in being too forward or too slow in making observations on the particular facts recorded in them.

There are those who are very assiduous in reading, and yet do not much advance their knowledge by it. They are delighted with the stories that are told, and perhaps can tell them again, for they make all they read nothing but history to themselves; but not reflecting on it, not making to themselves observations from what they read, they are very little improved by all that crowd of particulars that either pass through or lodge themselves in their understandings. They dream on in a constant course of reading and cramming themselves, but, not digesting any thing, it produces nothing but a heap of crudities.

If their memories retain well, one may say they have the materials of knowledge, but, like those for building, they are of no advantage, if there be no other use made of them but to let them lie heaped up together. Opposite to these there are others who lose the improvement they should make of matters of fact by a quite contrary conduct. They are apt to draw general conclusions, and raise axioms from every particular they meet with. These make as little true benefit of history as the other, nay, being of forward and active spirits, receive more harm by it ; it being of worse consequence to steer one's thoughts by a wrong rule than to have none at all, error doing to busy men much more harm than ignorance to the slow and sluggish. Between these, those seem to do best who taking material and useful hints, sometimes from single matters of fact, carry them in their minds to be judged of by what they shall find in history to confirm or reverse these imperfect observations; which may be established into rules fit to be relied on, when they are justified by a sufficient and wary induction of particulars. He that makes no such reflections on what he reads, only loads his mind with a rhapsody of tales fit in winter nights for the entertainment of others ; and he that will improve every matter of fact into a maxim, will abound in contrary observations, that can be of no other use but to perplex and pudder him, if he compares them, or else to misguide him, if he gives himself up to the authority of that which for its novelty, or for some other fancy, best pleases him.

SECTION XIV.

BIAS.

Next to these we may place those who suffer their own natural tempers and passions they are possessed with to influence their judgments, especially of men and things that may any way relate to their present circumstances and interest. Truth is all simple, all pure, will bear no mixture of any thing else with it. It is rigid and inflexible to any bye interests; and so should the understanding be, whose use and excellency lies in conforming itself to it. To think of every thing just as it is in itself is the proper business of the understanding, though it be not that which men always employ it to. This all men, at first hearing, allow is the right use every one should make of his understanding. No body will be at such an open defiance with common sense, as to profess that we should not endeavour to know and think of things as they are in themselves, and yet there is nothing more frequent than to do the contrary. And men are apt to excuse themselves, and think they have reason to do so, if they have but a pretence that it is for God, or a good cause, that is, in effect, for themselves, their own persuasion, or party; for †to† those in their turns the several sects of men, especially in matters of religion, entitle God and a good cause. But God requires not men to wrong or misuse their faculties for Him, nor to lie to others or themselves for his sake; which they purposely do, who will not suffer their understandings to have right conceptions of the things proposed to them, and designedly restrain themselves from having just thoughts of every thing, as far as they are concerned to enquire. And as for a good cause, that needs not such ill helps, if it be good, truth will support it, and it has no need of fallacy or falsehood.

SECTION XV.

ARGUMENTS.

Very much of kin to this is the hunting after arguments to make good one side of a question, and wholly to neglect and refuse those which favour the other side.

What is this but wilfully to misguide the understanding?
And [it] is so far from giving truth its due value, that
it wholly debases it. [Men] espouse opinions that best
comport with their power, profit, or credit, and then seek
arguments to support them. Truth, light upon this way,
is of no more avail to us than error; for what is so taken
up by us may be false as well as true, and he has not
done his duty who has thus stumbled upon truth in his
way to preferment.

There is another, but more innocent way of collecting
arguments, very familiar among bookish men, which is to
furnish themselves with the arguments they meet with pro
and con in the questions they study. This helps them
not to judge right, nor argue strongly, but only to talk
copiously on either side, without being steady and settled
in their own judgments: for such arguments gathered
from other men's thoughts, floating only in the memory,
are there ready indeed to supply copious talk with some
appearance of reason, but are far from helping us to judge
right. Such variety of arguments only distract the understanding that relies on them, unless it has gone farther
than such a superficial way of examining; this is to quit
truth for appearance, only to serve our vanity. The
sure and only way to get true knowledge is to form in
our minds clear settled notions of things, with names annexed to those determined ideas. These we are to consider, and with their several relations and habitudes, and
not amuse ourselves with floating names, and words of
indetermined signification, which we can use in several
senses to serve a turn. It is in the perception of the
habitudes and respects our ideas have one to another that
real knowledge consists; and when a man once perceives
how far they agree or disagree one with another, he will

be able to judge of what other people say, and will not need
to be led by the arguments of others, which are many of
them nothing but plausible sophistry.   This will teach
him to state the question right, and see whereon it turns ;
and thus he will stand upon his own legs, and know by
his own understanding.   Whereas by collecting and learning arguments by heart, he will be but a retainer to
others ; and when any one questions the foundations they
are built upon, he will be at a nonplus, and be fain to give
up his implicit knowledge.

SECTION XVI.

HASTE.

Labour for labour['s] sake is against nature.   The
understanding, as well as all the other faculties, chooses
always the shortest way to its end, would presently obtain
the knowledge it is about, and then set upon some new
inquiry.   But this whether laziness or haste often misleads it, and makes it content itself with improper ways of
search and such as will not serve the turn.   Sometimes it
rests upon testimony, when testimony of right has nothing
to do, because it is easier to believe than to be scientifically
instructed.   Sometimes it contents itself with one argument, and rests satisfied with that, as it were a demonstration ; whereas the thing under proof is not capable of
demonstration, and therefore must be submitted to the trial
of probabilities, and all the material arguments pro and con
be examined and brought to a balance.   In some cases
the mind is determined by probable topics in inquiries,
where demonstration may be had.   All these, and several
others, which laziness, impatience, custom, and want of
use and attention lead men into, are misapplications of the
understanding in the search of truth.   In every question,

the nature and manner of the proof it is capable of should first be considered to make our inquiry such as it should be. This would save a great deal of frequently misemployed pains, and lead us sooner to that discovery and possession of truth we are capable of. The multiplying variety of arguments, especially frivolous ones, such as are all that are merely verbal, is not only lost labour, but cumbers the memory to no purpose, and serves only to hinder it from seizing and holding of the truth in all those cases which are capable of demonstration. In such a way of proof the truth and certainty is seen, and the mind fully possesses itself of it; when in the other way of assent, it only hovers about it, is amused with uncertainties. In this superficial way, indeed, the mind is capable of more variety of plausible talk, but is not enlarged as it should be in its knowledge. It is to this same haste and impatience of the mind also that a not due tracing of the arguments to their true foundation is owing; men see a little, presume a great deal, and so jump to the conclusion. This is a short way to fancy and conceit, and (if firmly embraced) to opiniatrity, but is certainly the farthest way about to knowledge. For he that will know must by the connection of the proofs see the truth, and the ground it stands on ; and, therefore, if he has for haste skipt over what he should have examined, he must begin and go over all again, or else he will never come to knowledge.

SECTION XVII.

DESULTORY.

Another fault of as ill consequence as this, which proceeds also from laziness with a mixture of vanity, is the skipping from one sort of knowledge to another. Some men's tempers are quickly weary of any one thing. Constancy and assiduity is what they cannot bear : the same study long continued in is as intolerable to them, as the appearing long in the same clothes or fashion is to a court lady.

SECTION XVIII.

SMATTERING.

Others, that they may seem universally knowing, get a little smattering in every thing. Both these may fill their heads with superficial notions of things, but are very much out of the way of attaining truth or knowledge.

SECTION XIX.

UNIVERSALITY.

I do not here speak against the taking a taste of every sort of knowledge ; it is certainly very useful and necessary to form the mind, but then it must be done in a different way and to a different end. Not for talk and vanity to fill the head with shreds of all kinds, that he, who is possessed of such a frippery, may be able to match the discourses of all he shall meet with, as if nothing could come amiss to him, and his head was so well stored a magazine, that nothing could be proposed which he was not master of and was readily furnished to entertain any one on. This is an excellency indeed, and a great one too, to have a real and true knowledge in all or most of the objects of contemplation. But it is what the mind of one and the same man can hardly attain unto ; and the instances are so few of those who have in any measure

approached towards it, that I know not whether they are
to be proposed as examples in the ordinary conduct of
the understanding. For a man to understand fully the
business of his particular calling in the commonwealth,
and of religion, which is his calling as he is a man in the
world, is usually enough to take up his whole time ; and
there are few that inform themselves in these, which is
every man's proper and peculiar business, so to the
bottom as they should do. But though this be so, and
there are very few men that extend their thoughts towards
universal knowledge, yet I do not doubt but if the right
way were taken, and the methods of enquiry were ordered
as they should be, men of little business and great leisure
might go a great deal farther in it than is usually done.
To return to the business in hand, the end and use of
a little insight in those parts of knowledge, which are not
a man's proper business, is to accustom our minds to all
sorts of ideas and the proper ways of examining their
habitudes and relations. This gives the mind a freedom,
and the exercising the understanding in the several ways
of inquiry and reasoning, which the most skilful have
made use of, teaches the mind sagacity and wariness, and
a suppleness to apply itself more closely and dexterously
to the bents and turns of the matter in all its researches.
Besides, this universal taste of all the sciences, with an
indifferency before the mind is possessed with any one in
particular and grown into love and admiration of what is
made its darling, will prevent another evil very commonly
to be observed in those who have from the beginning
been seasoned only by one part of knowledge. Let a
man be given up to the contemplation of one sort of
knowledge, and that will become every thing. The mind
will take such a tincture from a familiarity with that

object, that every thing else, how remote soever, will be brought under the same view. A metaphysician will bring plowing and gardening immediately to abstract notions; the history of nature shall signify nothing to him. An alchymist, on the contrary, shall reduce divinity to the maxims of his laboratory, explain morality by Sal, Sulphur, and Mercury, and allegorize the scripture itself, and the sacred mysteries thereof, into the philosopher's stone. And I heard once a man, who had a more than ordinary excellency in music, seriously accommodate Moses' seven days of the first week to the notes of music, as if from thence had been taken the measure and method of the creation. It is of no small consequence to keep the mind from such a possession, which I think is best done by giving it a fair and equal view of the whole intellectual world, wherein it may see the order, rank, and beauty of the whole, and give a just allowance to the distinct provinces of the several sciences in the due order and usefulness of each of them.

If this be that which old men will not think necessary, nor be easily brought to, it is fit at least that it should be practised in the breeding of the young. The business of education, as I have already observed, is not, as I think, to make them perfect in any one of the sciences, but so to open and dispose their minds as may best make them capable of any, when they shall apply themselves to it. If men are for a long time accustomed only to one sort or method of thoughts, their minds grow stiff in it, and do not readily turn to another. It is therefore to give them this freedom, that I think they should be made to look into all sorts of knowledge, and exercise their understandings in so wide a variety and stock of knowledge. But I do not propose it as a variety and stock of knowledge, but a variety and freedom of thinking, as an increase of the powers and activity of the mind, not as an enlargement of its possessions.

SECTION XX.

READING.

This is that which I think great readers are apt to be mistaken in. Those who have read of every thing are thought to understand every thing too; but it is not always so. Reading furnishes the mind only with materials of knowledge; it is thinking makes what we read ours. We are of the ruminating kind, and it is not enough to cram ourselves with a great load of collections; unless we chew them over again, they will not give us strength and nourishment. There are indeed in some writers visible instances of deep thoughts, close and acute reasoning, and ideas well pursued. The light these would give, would be of great use, if their readers would observe and imitate them; all the rest at best are but particulars fit to be turned into knowledge, but that can be done only by our own meditation, and examining the reach, force, and coherence of what is said; and then, as far as we apprehend and see the connection of ideas, so far it is ours; without that, it is but so much loose matter floating in our brain. The memory may be stored, but the judgment is little better, and the stock of knowledge not increased, by being able to repeat what others have said or produce the arguments we have found in them. Such a knowledge as this is but knowledge by hearsay, and the ostentation of it is at best but talking by rote, and very often upon weak and wrong

principles. For all that is to be found in books is not
built upon true foundations, nor always rightly deduced
from the principles it is pretended to be built on. Such
an examen as is requisite to discover that, every reader's
mind is not forward to make ; especially in those who
have given themselves up to a party, and only hunt for
what they can scrape together that may favour and support the tenets of it. Such men wilfully exclude themselves from truth and from all true benefit to be received
by reading. Others of more indifferency often want
attention and industry. The mind is backward in itself
to be at the pains to trace every argument to its original,
and to see upon what basis it stands, and how firmly ;
but yet it is this that gives so much the advantage to one
man more than another in reading. The mind should,
by severe rules, be tied down to this at first uneasy task ;
use and exercise will give it facility. So that those who
are accustomed to it, readily, as it were with one cast of
the eye, take a view of the argument, and presently, in
most cases, see where it bottoms. Those who have got
this faculty, one may say, have got the true key of books,
and the clue to lead them through the mizmaze of variety
of opinions and authors to truth and certainty. This
young beginners should be entered in, and shewed the
use of, that they might profit by their reading. Those
who are strangers to it will be apt to think it too great
a clog in the way of men's studies, and they will suspect
they shall make but small progress, if, in the books they
read, they must stand to examine and unravel every argument and follow it step by step up to its original.

I answer, this is a good objection, and ought to weigh
with those whose reading is designed for much talk and
little knowledge, and I have nothing to say to it. But

I am here inquiring into the conduct of the understanding in its progress towards knowledge; and to those who aim at that, I may say that he, who fair and softly goes steadily forward in a course that points right, will sooner be at his journey's end, than he that runs after every one he meets, though he gallop all day full speed.

To which let me add, that this way of thinking on and profiting by what we read will be a clog and rub to any one only in the beginning; when custom and exercise has made it familiar, it will be dispatched in most occasions, without resting or interruption in the course of our reading. The motions and views of a mind exercised that way are wonderfully quick; and a man, used to such sort of reflections, sees as much at one glimpse as would require a long discourse to lay before another and make out in an entire and gradual deduction. Besides, that when the first difficulties are over, the delight and sensible advantage it brings mightily encourages and enlivens the mind in reading, which without this is very improperly called study.

SECTION XXI.

INTERMEDIATE PRINCIPLES.

As an help to this, I think it may be proposed that, for the saving the long progression of the thoughts to remote and first principles in every case, the mind should provide itself several stages; that is to say, intermediate principles, which it might have recourse to in the examining those positions that come in its way. These, though they are not self-evident principles, yet, if they have been made out from them by a wary and unquestionable deduction, may be depended on as certain and infallible truths, and serve as unquestionable truths to prove other points depending on them by a nearer and shorter view than remote and general maxims. These may serve as landmarks to shew what lies in the direct way of truth, or is quite besides it. And thus mathematicians do, who do not in every new problem run it back to the first axioms, through all the whole train of intermediate propositions. Certain theorems, that they have settled to themselves upon sure demonstration, serve to resolve to them multitudes of propositions which depend on them, and are as firmly made out from thence, as if the mind went afresh over every link of the whole chain that ties them to first self-evident principles. Only in other sciences great care is to be taken that they establish those intermediate principles with as much caution, exactness, and indifferency, as mathematicians use in the settling any of their great theorems. When this is not done, but men take up the principles in this or that science upon credit, inclination, interest, &c. in haste, without due examination and most unquestionable proof, they lay a trap for themselves, and as much as in them lies captivate their understandings to mistake, falsehood, and error.

SECTION XXII.

PARTIALITY.

As there is a partiality to opinions, which, as we have already observed, is apt to mislead the understanding, so there is often a partiality to studies, which is prejudicial also to knowledge and improvement. Those sciences

which men are particularly versed in they are apt to value
and extol, as if that part of knowledge which every one
has acquainted himself with were that alone which was
worth the having, and all the rest were idle and empty
amusements, comparatively of no use or importance.
This is the effect of ignorance and not knowledge, the
being vainly puffed up with a flatulency arising from
a weak and narrow comprehension. It is not amiss that
every one should relish the science that he has made his
peculiar study; a view of its beauties and a sense of its
usefulness carries a man on with the more delight and
warmth in the pursuit and improvement of it. But the
contempt of all other knowledge, as if it were nothing in
comparison of law or physic, of astronomy or chymistry,
or perhaps some yet meaner part of knowledge, wherein
I have got some smattering, or am somewhat advanced,
is not only the mark of a vain or little mind, but does
this prejudice in the conduct of the understanding, that
it coops it up within narrow bounds, and hinders it from
looking abroad into other provinces of the intellectual
world, more beautiful possibly, and more fruitful than
that which it had till then laboured in ; wherein it might
find, besides new knowledge, ways or hints whereby it
might be enabled the better to cultivate its own.

SECTION XXIII.

THEOLOGY.

There is indeed one science (as they are now distinguished) incomparably above all the rest, where it is
not by corruption narrowed into a trade or faction, for
mean or ill ends and secular interests; I mean theology,

which, containing the knowledge of God and His creatures, our duty to him and our fellow-creatures, and a
view of our present and future state, is the comprehension of all other knowledge directed to its true end, i.e.
the honour and veneration of the Creator and the happi-
ness of mankind. This is that noble study which is
every man's duty, and every one that can be called a
rational creature is capable of. The works of nature
and the words of revelation display it to mankind in
characters so large and visible, that those who are not
quite blind may in them read and see the first principles
and most necessary parts of it; and from thence, as they
have time and industry, may be enabled to go on to the
more abstruse parts of it, and penetrate into those infinite
depths filled with the treasures of wisdom and knowledge.
This is that science which would truly enlarge men's
minds, were it studied, or permitted to be studied, every
where with that freedom, love of truth and charity, which
it teaches, and were not made, contrary to its nature, the
occasion of strife, faction, malignity, and narrow impo-
sitions. I shall say no more here of this, but that it
is undoubtedly a wrong use of my understanding to make
it the rule and measure of another man's; a use which
it is neither fit for nor capable of.

SECTION XXIV.

PARTIALITY.

This partiality, where it is not permitted an authority to
render all other studies insignificant or contemptible, is
often indulged so far as to be relied upon and made use
of in other parts of knowledge, to which it does not at all
belong, and wherewith it has no manner of affinity. Some

men have so used their heads to mathematical figures that, giving a preference to the methods of that science, they introduce lines and diagrams into their study of divinity or politic enquiries, as if nothing could be known without them; and others, accustomed to retired speculations, run natural philosophy into metaphysical notions and the abstract generalities of logic; and how often may one meet with religion and morality treated of in the terms of the laboratory, and thought to be improved by the methods and notions of chymistry. But he that will take care of the conduct of his understanding, to direct it right to the knowledge of things, must avoid those undue mixtures, and not by a fondness for what he has found useful and necessary in one transfer it to another science, where it serves only to perplex and confound the understanding. It is a certain truth that *res nolunt male administrari*; it is no less certain, *res nolunt male intelligi.* Things themselves are to be considered as they are in themselves, and then they will shew us in what way they are to be understood. For to have right conceptions about them, we must bring our understandings to the inflexible natures and unalterable relations of things, and not endeavour to bring things to any preconceived notions of our own.

There is another partiality very commonly observable in men of study, no less prejudicial nor ridiculous than the former; and that is a fantastical and wild attributing all knowledge to the ancients alone, or to the moderns. This raving upon antiquity in matter of poetry, Horace has wittily described and exposed in one of his satyrs. The same sort of madness may be found in reference to all the other sciences. Some will not admit an opinion not authorized by men of old, who were then all giants in knowledge : nothing is to be put into the treasury of

truth or knowledge, which has not the stamp of Greece or
Rome upon it ; and since their days will scarce allow that
men have been able to see, think, or write.   Others, with
a like extravagancy, contemn all that the ancients have left
us, and, being taken with the modern inventions and discoveries, lay by all that went before, as if whatever is
called old must have the decay of time upon it, and truth
too were liable to mould and rottenness.   Men, I think,
have been much the same for natural endowments in all
times.   Fashion, discipline, and education have put eminent differences in the ages of several countries, and made
one generation much differ from another in arts and
sciences : but truth is always the same ; time alters it not,
nor is it the better or worse for being of ancient or modern
tradition.   Many were eminent in former ages of the
world for their discovery and delivery of it ; but though
the knowledge they have left us be worth our study, yet
they exhausted not all its treasure ; they left a great deal
for the industry and sagacity of after ages, and so shall we.
That was once new to them which any one now receives
with veneration for its antiquity ; nor was it the worse
for appearing as a novelty, and that which is now embraced for its newness will, to posterity, be old, but not
thereby be less true or less genuine.   There is no occasion
on this account to oppose the ancients and the moderns
to one another, or to be squeamish on either side.   He
that wisely conducts his mind in the pursuit of knowledge
will gather what lights, and get what helps he can, from
either of them, from whom they are best to be had,
without adoring the errors or rejecting the truths which
he may find mingled in them.

Another partiality may be observed, in some to vulgar,
in others to heterodox tenets : some are apt to conclude

that what is the common opinion cannot but be true ; so
many men's eyes they think cannot but see right ; so many
men's understandings of all sorts cannot be deceived,
and therefore [they] will not venture to look beyond the
received notions of the place and age, nor have so pre-
sumptuous a thought as to be wiser than their neighbours.
They are content to go with the crowd, and so go easily,
which they think is going right, or at least serves them as
well. But however *vox populi vox Dei* has prevailed as
a maxim, yet I do not remember wherever God delivered
his oracles by the multitude, or Nature truths by the herd.
On the other side, some fly all common opinions as either
false or frivolous. The title of many-headed beast is
a sufficient reason to them to conclude that no truths of
weight or consequence can be lodged there. Vulgar
opinions are suited to vulgar capacities, and adapted to
the ends of those that govern. He that will know the
truth of things must leave the common and beaten track,
which none but weak and servile minds are satisfied to
trudge along continually in. Such nice palates relish
nothing but strange notions quite out of the way : whatever is commonly received has the mark of the beast on
it, and they think it a lessening to them to hearken to it,
or receive it ; their mind runs only after paradoxes ;
these they seek, these they embrace, these alone they
vent, and so, as they think, distinguish themselves from
the vulgar. But common or uncommon are not the
marks to distinguish truth or falsehood, and therefore
should not be any bias to us in our enquiries. We should
not judge of things by men's opinions, but of opinions by
things. The multitude reason but ill, and therefore may
be well suspected, and cannot be relied on, nor should
be followed as a sure guide ; but philosophers who have

quitted the orthodoxy of the community, and the populaı doctrines of their countries, have fallen into as extravagant and as absurd opinions as ever common reception countenanced. It would be madness to refuse to breathe the common air, or quench one's thirst with water, because the rabble use them to these purposes; and, if there are conveniences of life which common use reaches not, it is not reason to reject them, because they are not grown into the ordinary fashion of the country, and every villager doth not know them.

Truth, whether in or out of fashion, is the measure of knowledge, and the business of the understanding; whatsoever is besides that, however authorized by consent or recommended by rarity, is nothing but ignorance, or something worse.

Another sort of partiality there is, whereby men impose upon themselves, and by it make their reading little useful to themselves; I mean the making use of the opinions of writers, and laying stress upon their authorities, wherever they find them to favour their own opinions.

There is nothing almost has done more harm to men dedicated to letters than giving the name of study to reading, and making a man of great reading to be the same with a man of great knowledge, or at least to be a title of honour. All that can be recorded in writing are only facts or reasonings. Facts are of three sorts :·

1. Merely of natural agents, observable in the ordinary operations of bodies one upon another, whether in the visible course of things left to themselves, or in experiments made by men applying agents and patients to one another, after a peculiar and artificial manner.

2. Of voluntary agents, more especially the actions of men in society, which makes civil and moral history.

3. Of opinions.

In these three consists, as it seems to me, that which commonly has the name of learning; to which perhaps some may add a distinct head of critical writings, which indeed at bottom is nothing but matter of fact, and resolves itself into this, that such a man, or set of men, used such a word or phrase in such a sense, i.e. that they made such sounds the marks of such ideas.

Under reasonings I comprehend all the discoveries of general truths made by human reason, whether found by intuition, demonstration, or probable deductions. And this is that which is, if not alone knowledge (because the truth or probability of particular propositions may be known too), yet is, as may be supposed, most properly the business of those who pretend to improve their understandings and make themselves knowing by reading.

Books and reading are looked upon to be the great helps of the understanding and instruments of knowledge, as it must be allowed that they are; and yet I beg leave to question whether these do not prove an hindrance to many, and keep several bookish men from attaining to solid and true knowledge. This, I think, I may be permitted to say, that there is no part wherein the understanding needs a more careful and wary conduct than in the use of books; without which they will prove rather innocent amusements than profitable employments of our time, and bring but small additions to our knowledge.

There is not seldom to be found even amongst those who aim at knowledge, who with an unwearied industry employ their whole time in books, who scarce allow themselves time to eat or sleep, but read, and read, and read on, but yet make no great advances in real knowledge, though there be no defect in their intellectual faculties, to which their little progress can be imputed. The mistake here is, that it is usually supposed that, by reading, the author's knowledge is transfused into the reader's understanding; and so it is, but not by bare reading, but by reading and understanding what he writ. Whereby I mean, not barely comprehending what is affirmed or denied in each proposition (though that great readers do not always think themselves concerned precisely to do), but to see and follow the train of his reasonings, observe the strength and clearness of their connection, and examine upon what they bottom. Without this, a man may read the discourses of a very rational author, writ in a language and in propositions that he very well understands, and yet acquire not one jot of his knowledge; which consisting only in the perceived, certain, or probable connection of the ideas made use of in his reasonings, the reader's knowledge is no farther increased than he perceives that, so much as he sees of this connection, so much he knows of the truth or probability of that author's opinions.

All that he relies on without this perception, he takes upon trust upon the author's credit, without any knowledge of it at all. This makes me not at all wonder to see some men so abound in citations, and build so much upon authorities, it being the sole foundation on which they bottom most of their own tenets; so that in effect they have but a second hand or implicit knowledge, i.e. are in the right, if such an one from whom they borrowed it were in the right in that opinion which they took from him, which indeed is no knowledge at all. Writers of this or former ages may be good witnesses of matters of fact which they deliver, which we may do well to take upon their authority; but their credit can go no farther than this, it cannot at all affect the truth and falsehood of opinions, which have no other sort of trial but reason and proof, which they themselves made use of to make themselves knowing, and so must others too that will partake in their knowledge. Indeed it is an advantage that they have been at the pains to find out the proofs, and lay them in that order that may shew the truth or probability of their conclusions; and for this we owe them great acknowledgments for saving us the pains in searching out those proofs which they have collected for us, and which possibly, after all our pains, we might not have found, nor been able to have set them in so good a light as that which they left them us in. Upon this account we are mightily beholding to judicious writers of all ages for those discoveries and discourses they have left behind them for our instruction, if we know how to make a right use of them; which is not to run them over in a hasty perusal, and perhaps lodge their opinions or some remarkable passages in our memories, but to enter into their reasonings, examine their proofs, and then judge of the truth or falsehood, probability or improbability of what they advance, not by any opinion we have entertained of the author, but by the evidence he produces and the conviction he affords us, drawn from things themselves. Knowing is seeing, and, if it be so, it is madness to persuade ourselves that we do so by another man's eyes, let him use ever so many words to tell us that what he asserts is very visible. Till we ourselves see it with our own eyes, and perceive it by our own understandings, we are as much in the dark and as void of knowledge as before, let us believe any learned author as much as we will.

Euclid and Archimedes are allowed to be knowing, and

to have demonstrated what they say; and yet, whoever shall read over their writings without perceiving the connection of their proofs, and seeing what they shew, though he may understand all their words, yet he is not the more knowing : he may believe indeed, but does not know what they say, and so is not advanced one jot in mathematical knowledge by all his reading of those approved mathematicians.

SECTION XXV.

HASTE.

The eagerness and strong bent of the mind after knowledge, if not warily regulated, is often an hindrance to it. It still presses into farther discoveries and new objects, and catches at the variety of knowledge, and therefore often stays not long enough on what is before it to look into it as it should, for haste to pursue what is yet out of sight. He that rides post through a country may be able, from the transient view, to tell how in general the parts lie, and may be able to give some loose description of here a mountain and there a plain, here a morass and there a river, woodland in one part and savanas in another. Such superficial ideas and observations as these he may collect in galloping over it. But the more useful observations of the soil, plants, animals, and inhabitants, with their several sorts and properties, must necessarily escape him ; and it is seldom men ever discover the rich mines, without some digging. Nature commonly lodges her treasure and jewels in rocky ground. If the matter be knotty, and the sense lies deep, the mind must stop and buckle to it, and stick upon it with labour and thought and close contemplation, and not leave it till it has mastered the difficulty, and got possession of truth. But here care must be taken to avoid the other extreme : a man must not stick at every useless nicety, and expect mysteries of science in every trivial question or scruple that he may raise. He that will stand to pick up and examine every pebble that comes in his way is as unlikely to return enriched and loaden with jewels, as the other that travelled full speed. Truths are not the better nor the worse for their obviousness or difficulty, but their value is to be measured by their usefulness and tendency. Insignificant observations should not take up any of our minutes, and those that enlarge our view, and give light towards farther and useful discoveries, should not be neglected, though they stop our course, and spend some of our time in a fixed attention.

There is another haste that does often and will mislead the mind, if it be left to itself and its own conduct. The understanding is naturally forward, not only to learn its knowledge by variety (which makes it skip over one to get speedily to another part of knowledge), but also eager to enlarge its views by running too fast into general observations and conclusions, without a due examination of particulars enough whereon to found those general axioms. This seems to enlarge their stock, but it is of fancies not realities ; such theories built upon narrow foundations stand but weakly, and, if they fall not of themselves, are at least very hard to be supported against the assaults of opposition. And thus men, being too hasty to erect to themselves general notions and ill-grounded theories, find themselves deceived in their stock of knowledge, when they come to examine their hastily assumed maxims themselves, or to have them attacked by others. General observations drawn from particulars are the jewels of knowledge, comprehending great store in a little room; but they are therefore to be made with the greater care and caution, lest, if we take counterfeit for true, our loss and shame be the greater when our stock comes to a severe scrutiny. One or two particulars may suggest hints of enquiry, and they do well who take those hints; but if they turn them into conclusions, and make them presently general rules, they are forward indeed, but it is only to impose on themselves by propositions assumed for truths without sufficient warrant. To make such observations is, as has been already remarked, to make the head a magazine of materials which can hardly be called knowledge, or at least it is but like a collection of lumber not reduced to use or order; and he that makes every thing an observation has the same useless plenty and much more falsehood mixed with it. The extremes on both sides are to be avoided, and he will be able to give the best account of his studies who keeps his understanding in the right mean between them.

SECTION XXVI.

ANTICIPATION.

Whether it be a love of that which brings the first light and information to their minds, and want of vigour and industry to enquire, or else that men content themselves with any appearance of knowledge, right or wrong, which, when they have once got, they will hold fast: this is visible, that many men give themselves up to the first anticipations of their minds, and are very tenacious of the opinions that first possess them; they are often as fond of their first conceptions as of their first born, and will by no means recede from the judgment they have once made, or any conjecture or conceit which they have once entertained. This is a fault in the conduct of the understanding, since this firmness or rather stiffness of the mind is not from an adherence to truth but a submission to prejudice. It is an unreasonable homage paid to prepossession, whereby we shew a reverence not to (what we pretend to seek) truth; but what by hap-hazard we chance to light on, be it what it will. This is visibly a preposterous use of our faculties, and is a downright prostituting of the mind to resign it thus, and put it under the power of the first comer. This can never be allowed or ought to be followed as a right way to knowledge, till the understanding (whose business it is to conform itself to what it finds on the objects without) can by its own opiniatry change that, and make the unalterable nature of things comply with its own hasty determinations, which will never be. Whatever we fancy, things keep their course; and their habitudes, correspondences, and relations keep the same to one another.

SECTION XXVII.

RESIGNATION.

Contrary to these, but by a like dangerous excess on the other side, are those who always resign their judgment to the last man they heard or read. Truth never sinks into these men's minds, nor gives any tincture to them, but, chameleon-like, they take the colour of what is laid before them, and as soon lose and resign it to the next that happens to come in their way. The order wherein opinions are proposed or received by us is no rule of their rectitude, nor ought to be a cause of their preference. First or last in this case is the effect of chance, and not the measure of truth or falsehood. This every one must confess, and therefore should, in the pursuit of truth, keep his mind free from the influence of any such accidents. A man may as reasonably draw cuts for his tenets, regulate his persuasion by the cast of a die, as take it up for its novelty, or retain it because it had his first assent and he was never of another mind. Well-weighed reasons are to determine the judgment; those the mind should be always ready to hearken and submit to, and by their testimony and suffrage entertain or reject any tenet indifferently, whether it be a perfect stranger or an old acquaintance.

SECTION XXVIII.

PRACTICE.

Though the faculties of the mind are improved by exercise, yet they must not be put to a stress beyond their strength. *Quid valeant humeri, quid ferre recusent*, must be made the measure of every one's understanding, who has a desire not only to perform well, but to keep up the vigour of his faculties, and not to balk his understanding by what is too hard for it. The mind by being engaged in a task beyond its strength, like the body strained by lifting at a weight too heavy, has often its force broken, and thereby gets an unaptness or an aversion to any vigorous attempt ever after. A sinew cracked seldom recovers its former strength, or at least the tenderness of the sprain remains a good while after, and the memory of it longer, and leaves a lasting caution in the man not to put the part quickly again to any robust employment. So it fares in the mind once jaded by an attempt above its power; it either is disabled for the future, or else checks at any vigorous undertaking ever after, at least is very hardly brought to exert its force again on any subject that requires thought and meditation. The understanding should be brought to the difficult and knotty parts of knowledge, that try the strength of thought and a full bent of the mind, by insensible degrees; and in such a gradual proceeding nothing is too hard for it. Nor let it be objected, that such a slow progress will never reach the extent of some sciences. It is not to be imagined how far constancy will carry a man; however, it is better walking slowly in a rugged way, than to break a leg and be a cripple. He that begins with the calf may carry the ox; but he that will at first go to take up an ox, may so disable himself, as not [to] be able to lift a calf after that. When the mind, by insensible degrees, has brought itself to attention and close thinking, it will be able to cope with difficulties, and master them without any prejudice to itself, and then it may go on roundly. Every abstruse problem, every intricate question will not baffle, discourage, or break it. But though putting the mind unprepared upon an unusual stress that may discourage or damp it for the future ought to be avoided, yet this must not run it, by an over great shyness of difficulties, into a lazy sauntering about ordinary and obvious things that demand no thought or application. This debases and enervates the understanding, makes it weak and unfit for labour. This is a sort of hovering about the surface of things, without any insight into them or penetration ; and, when the mind has been once habituated to this lazy recumbency and satisfaction on the obvious surface of things, it is in danger to rest satisfied there, and go no deeper, since it cannot do it without pains and digging. He that has for some time accustomed himself to take up with what easily offers itself at first view, has reason to fear he shall never reconcile himself to the fatigue of turning and tumbling things in his mind to discover their more retired and more valuable secrets.

It is not strange that methods of learning, which scholars have been accustomed to in their beginning and entrance upon the sciences, should influence them all their lives, and be settled in their minds by an overruling reverence, especially if they be such as universal use has established. Learners must at first be believers, and, their masters' rules having been once made axioms to them, it is no wonder they should keep that dignity, and, by the authority they have once got, mislead those who think it sufficient to excuse them, if they go out of their way in a well beaten track.

SECTION XXIX.

WORDS.

I have copiously enough spoken of the abuse of words in another place, and therefore shall upon this reflection, that the sciences are full of them, warn those that would conduct their understandings right, not to take any term, howsoever authorized by the language of the schools, to stand for any thing till they have an idea of it. A word may be of frequent use and great credit with several authors, and be by them made use of, as if it stood for some real being; but yet if he that reads cannot frame any distinct idea of that being, it is certainly to him a mere empty sound without a meaning, and he learns no more by all that is said of it or attributed to it, than if it were affirmed only of that bare empty sound. They who would advance in knowledge, and not deceive and swell themselves with a little articulated air, should lay down this as a fundamental rule, not to take words for things, nor suppose that names in books signify real entities in nature, till they can frame clear and distinct ideas of those entities. It will not perhaps be allowed if I should set down *substantial forms* and *intentional species*, as such that may justly be suspected to be of this kind of insignificant terms. But this I am sure, to one that can form no determined ideas of what they stand for, they signify nothing at all; and all that he thinks he knows about them is to him so much knowledge about nothing, and amounts at most but to a learned ignorance. It is not without all reason supposed, that there are many such empty terms to be found in some learned writers, to which they had recourse to etch out their systems where their understandings could not furnish them with conceptions from things. But yet I believe the supposing of some realities in nature, answering those and the like words, have much perplexed some, and quite misled others in the study of nature. That which in any discourse signifies, *I know not what*, should be considered *I know not when*. Where men have any conceptions, they can, if they are ever so abstruse or abstracted, explain them, and the terms they use for them. For our conceptions being nothing but ideas, which are all made up of simple ones, if they cannot give us the ideas their words stand for, it is plain they have none. To what purpose can it be to hunt after his conceptions, who has none, or none distinct? He that knew not what he himself meant by a learned term, cannot make us know any thing by his use of it, let us beat our heads about it ever so long. Whether we are able to comprehend all the operations of nature and the manners of them, it matters not to enquire; but this is certain, that we can comprehend no more of them than we can distinctly conceive; and therefore to obtrude terms where we have no distinct conceptions, as if they did contain or rather conceal something, is but an artifice of learned vanity, to cover a defect in an hypothesis or our understandings. Words are not made to conceal, but to declare and shew something; where they are by those, who pretend to instruct, otherwise used, they conceal indeed something, but that which they conceal is nothing but the ignorance, error, or sophistry of the talker, for there is, in truth, nothing else under them.

SECTION XXX.

WANDERING.

That there is a constant succession and flux of ideas in our minds, I have observed in the former part of this essay, and every one may take notice of it in himself. This I suppose may deserve some part of our care in the conduct of our understandings; and I think it may be of great advantage, if we can by use get that power over our minds as to be able to direct that train of ideas, that so, since there will new ones perpetually come into our thoughts by a constant succession, we may be able by choice so to direct them, that none may come in view, but such as are pertinent to our present enquiry, and in such order as may be most useful to the discovery we are upon ; or at least, if some foreign and unsought ideas will offer themselves, that yet we might be able to reject them, and keep them from taking off our minds from its present pursuit, and hinder them from running away with our thoughts quite from the subject in hand. This is not, I suspect, so easy to be done as perhaps may be imagined; and yet, for aught I know, this may be, if not the chief, yet one of the great differences that carry some men in their reasoning so far beyond others, where they seem to be naturally of equal parts. A proper and effectual remedy for this wandering of thoughts I would be glad to find. He that shall propose such an one would do great service to the studious and contemplative part of mankind, and perhaps help unthinking men to become thinking. I must acknowledge that hitherto I have discovered no other way to keep our thoughts close to their business, but the endeavouring as much as we can, and by frequent attention and application getting the habit of attention and application. He that will observe children, will find that, even when they endeavour their uttermost, they cannot keep their minds from straggling. The way to cure it, I am satisfied, is not angry chiding or beating, for that presently fills their heads with all the ideas that fear, dread, or confusion can offer to them. To bring back gently their wandering thoughts, by leading them into the path and going before them in the train they should pursue, without any rebuke, or so much as taking notice (where it can be avoided) of their roving, I suppose would sooner reconcile and inure them to attention, than all those rougher methods which more distract their thought, and, hindering the application they would promote, introduce a contrary habit.

SECTION XXXI.

DISTINCTION.

Distinction and division are (if I mistake not the import of the words) very different things : the one being the perception of a difference that nature has placed in things; the other our making a division where there is yet none. At least, if I may be permitted to consider them in this sense, I think I may say of them, that one of them is the most necessary and conducive to true knowledge that can be, the other, when too much made use of, serves only to puzzle and confound the understanding. To observe every the least difference that is in things argues a quick and clear sight, and this keeps the understanding steady and right in its way to knowledge. But though it be useful to discern every variety that is to be found in nature, yet it is not convenient to consider every difference that is in things, and divide them into distinct classes under every such difference. This will run us, if followed, into particulars (for every individual has something that differences it from another), and we shall be able to establish no general truths, or else at least shall be apt to perplex the mind about them. The collection of several things into several classes gives the mind more general and larger views; but we must take care to unite them only in that and so far as they do agree, for so far they may be united under the consideration. For entity itself, that comprehends all things, as general as it is, may afford us clear and rational conceptions. If we would well weigh and keep in our minds what it is we are considering, that would best instruct us when we should or should not branch into farther distinctions, which are to be taken only from a due contemplation of things; to which there is nothing more opposite than the art of verbal distinctions, made at pleasure, in learned and arbitrarily invented terms to be applied at a venture, without comprehending or conveying any distinct notions, and so altogether fitted to artificial talk or empty noise in dispute, without any clearing of difficulties or advance in knowledge. Whatsoever subject we examine and would get knowledge in, we should, I think, make as general and as large as it will bear; nor can there be any danger of this, if the idea of it be settled and determined: for, if that be so, we shall easily distinguish it from any other idea, though comprehended under the same name. For it is to fence against the entanglements of equivocal words, and the great art of sophistry which lies in them, that distinctions have been multiplied, and their use thought necessary. But had every distinct abstract idea a distinct known name, there would be little need of these multiplied scholastic distinctions, though there would be nevertheless as much need still of the mind's observing the differences that are in things, and discriminating them thereby one from another. It is not therefore the right way to knowledge, to hunt after, and fill the head with, abundance of artificial and scholastic distinctions, wherewith learned men's writings are often filled; and we

sometimes find what they treat of so divided and sub-
divided, that the mind of the most attentive reader loses
the sight of it, as it is more than probable the writer
himself did; for in things crumbled into dust it is in vain
to affect or pretend order, or expect clearness. To avoid
confusion by too few or too many divisions, is a great
skill in thinking as well as writing, which is but the copy-
ing our thoughts; but what are the boundaries of the
mean between the two vicious excesses on both hands,
I think is hard to set down in words: clear and distinct
ideas is all that I yet know able to regulate it. But as to
verbal distinctions received and applied to common terms,
i.e. equivocal words, they are more properly, I think, the
business of criticism and dictionaries than of real knowledge and philosophy, since they, for the most part,
explain the meaning of words, and give us their several
significations. The dexterous management of terms, and
being able to *fend* and *prove* with them, I know has and
does pass in the world for a great part of learning; but it
is learning distinct from knowledge, for knowledge consists only in perceiving the habitudes and relations of
ideas one to another, which is done without words; the
intervention of a sound helps nothing to it. And hence
we see that there is least use of distinctions where there is
most knowledge; I mean in mathematics, where men
have determined ideas with known names to them; and
so, there being no room for equivocations, there is no
need of distinctions. In arguing, the opponent uses as
comprehensive and equivocal terms as he can, to involve
his adversary in the doubtfulness of his expressions: this
is expected, and therefore the answerer on his side makes
it his play to distinguish as much as he can, and thinks
he can never do it too much; nor can he indeed in that

way wherein victory may be had without truth and without knowledge. This seems to me to be the art of
disputing. Use your words as captiously as you can in
your arguing on one side, and apply distinctions as much
as you can, on the other side, to every term, to nonplus
your opponent; so that in this sort of scholarship, there
being no bounds set to distinguishing, some men have
thought all acuteness to have lain in it; and therefore in
all they have read or thought on, their great business has
been to amuse themselves with distinctions, and multiply
to themselves divisions, at least more than the nature of
the thing required. There seems to me, as I said, to be
no other rule for this, but a due and right consideration
of things as they are in themselves. He that has settled
in his mind determined ideas, with names affixed to them.
will be able both to discern their differences one from
another, which is really distinguishing; and, where the
penury of words affords not terms answering every distinct idea, will be able to apply proper distinguishing
terms to the comprehensive and equivocal names he is
forced to make use of. This is all the need I know of
distinguishing terms; and, in such verbal distinctions,
each term of the distinction, joined to that whose signification it distinguishes, is but a new distinct name for a distinct idea. Where they are so, and men have clear and distinct conceptions that answer their verbal distinctions,
they are right, and are pertinent as far as they serve to
clear any thing in the subject under consideration. And
this is that which seems to me the proper and only
measure of distinctions and divisions; which he that will
conduct his understanding right must not look for in the
acuteness of invention, nor the authority of writers, but
will find only in the consideration of things themselves,

whether they are led into it by their own meditations or the information of books.

An aptness to jumble things together, wherein can be found any likeness, is a fault in the understanding on the other side, which will not fail to mislead it, and, by thus lumping of things, hinder the mind from distinct and accurate conceptions of them.

SECTION XXXII.

SIMILES.

To which let me here add another near of kin to this, at least in name, and that is, letting the mind, upon the suggestion of any new notion, run immediately after similes to make it the clearer to itself; which, though it may be a good way and useful in the explaining our thoughts to others, yet it is by no means a right method to settle true notions of any thing in ourselves, because similes always fail in some part, and come short of that exactness which our conceptions should have to things, if we would think aright. This indeed makes men plausible talkers; for those are always most acceptable in discourse, who have the way to let in their thoughts into other men's minds with the greatest ease and facility. Whether those thoughts are well formed and correspond with things, matters not; few men care to be instructed but at an easy rate. They who in their discourse strike the fancy, and take the hearers' conceptions along with them as fast as their words flow, are the applauded talkers, and go for the only men of clear thoughts. Nothing contributes so much to this as similes, whereby men think they themselves understand better, because they are the better understood. But it is one thing to think right, and another thing to know the right way to lay our thoughts before others with advantage and clearness, be they right or wrong. Well chosen similes, metaphors and allegories, with method and order, do this the best of any thing, because, being taken from objects already known and familiar to the understanding, they are conceived as fast as spoken; and, the correspondence being concluded, the thing they are brought to explain and elucidate is thought to be understood too. Thus fancy passes for knowledge, and what is prettily said is mistaken for solid. I say not this to decry metaphor, or with design to take away that ornament of speech; my business here is not with rhetoricians and orators, but with philosophers and lovers of truth; to whom I would beg leave to give this one rule whereby to try whether, in the application of their thoughts to any thing for the improvement of their knowledge, they do in truth comprehend the matter before them really such as it is in itself. The way to discover this is to observe whether, in the laying it before themselves or others, they make use only of borrowed representations and ideas foreign to the thing, which are applied to it by way of accommodation, as bearing some proportion or imagined likeness to the subject under consideration. Figured and metaphorical expressions do well to illustrate more abstruse and unfamiliar ideas which the mind is not yet thoroughly accustomed to; but then they must be made use of to illustrate ideas that we already have, not to paint to us those which we yet have not. Such borrowed and allusive ideas may follow real and solid truth, to set it off when found, but must by no means be set in its place and taken for it. If all our search has yet reached no farther than simile and metaphor, we may assure ourselves we rather fancy than know, and are not yet penetrated into the inside and reality of the thing, be it what it will, but content ourselves with what our imaginations, not things themselves, furnish us with.

SECTION XXXIII.

ASSENT.

In the whole conduct of the understanding, there is nothing of more'moment than to know when, and where, and how far to give assent, and possibly there is nothing harder. It is very easily said, and no body questions it, that giving and withholding our assent, and the degrees of it, should be regulated by the evidence which things carry with them; and yet we see men are not the better for this rule; some firmly embrace doctrines upon slight grounds, some upon no grounds, and some contrary to appearance. Some admit of certainty, and are not to be moved in what they hold: others waver in every thing, and there want not those that reject all as uncertain. What then shall a novice, an enquirer, a stranger do in the case? I answer, use his eyes. There is a correspondence in things, and agreement and disagreement in ideas, discernible in very different degrees, and there are eyes in men to see them if they please, only their eyes may be dimmed or dazzled, and the discerning sight in them impaired or lost. Interest and passion dazzle, the custom of arguing on any side, even against our persuasions, dims the understanding, and makes it by degrees lose the faculty of discerning clearly between truth and falsehood, and so of adhering to the right side.

It is not safe to play with error, and dress it up to ourselves or others in the shape of truth. The mind by degrees loses its natural relish of real solid truth, is reconciled insensibly to any thing that can but be dressed up into any faint appearance of it; and, if the fancy be allowed the place of judgment at first in sport, it afterwards comes by use to usurp it, and what is recommended by this flatterer (that studies but to please) is received for good. There are so many ways of fallacy, such arts of giving colours, appearances, and resemblances by this court dresser, the fancy, that he who is not wary to admit nothing but truth itself, very careful not to make his mind subservient to any thing else, cannot but be caught. He that has a mind to believe, has half assented already; and he that, by often arguing against his own sense, imposes falsehoods on others, is not far from believing himself. This takes away the great distance there is betwixt truth and falsehood; it brings them almost together, and makes it no great odds, in things that approach so near, which you take; and when things are brought to that pass, passion or interest, &c. easily, and without being perceived, determine which shall be the right.

SECTION XXXIV.

INDIFFERENCY.

I have said above that we should keep a perfect indifferency for all opinions, not wish any of them true, or try to make them appear so; but, being indifferent, receive and embrace them according as evidence, and that alone,

gives the attestation of truth. They that do thus, i.e.
keep their minds indifferent to opinions, to be determined
only by evidence, will always find the understanding has
perception enough to distinguish between evidence or no
evidence, betwixt plain and doubtful; and if they neither
give nor refuse their assent but by that measure, they will
be safe in the opinions they have. Which being perhaps
but few, this caution will have also this good in it, that it
will put them upon considering, and teach them the
necessity of examining more than they do; without which
the mind is but a receptacle of inconsistences, not the
storehouse of truths. They that do not keep up this
indifferency in themselves for all but truth, not supposed,
but evidenced in themselves, put coloured spectacles
before their eyes, and look on things through false
glasses, and then think themselves excused in following
the false appearances, which they themselves put upon
them. I do not expect that by this way the assent should
in every one be proportioned to the grounds and clearness wherewith every truth is capable to be made out, or
that men should be perfectly kept from error: that is
more than human nature can by any means be advanced
to. I aim at no such unattainable privilege. I am only
speaking of what they should do who would deal fairly
with their own minds, and make a right use of their
faculties in the pursuit of truth. We fail them a great deal
more than they fail us. It is mismanagement more than
want of abilities that men have reason to complain of,
and which they actually do complain of in those that
differ from them. He that, by an indifferency for all but
truth, suffers not his assent to go faster than his evidence,
nor beyond it, will learn to examine and examine fairly
instead of presuming, and no body will be at a loss or in

danger for want of embracing those truths which are necessary in his station and circumstances. In any other way but this, all the world are born to orthodoxy: they imbibe at first the allowed opinions of their country and party, and so, never questioning their truth, not one of a hundred ever examines. They are applauded for presuming they are in the right. He that considers is a foe to orthodoxy, because possibly he may deviate from some of the received doctrines there. And thus men, without any industry or acquisition of their own, inherit local truths (for it is not the same every where), and are inured to assent without evidence. This influences farther than is thought; for what one of a hundred of the zéalous bigots in all parties ever examined the tenets he is so stiff in, or ever thought it his business or duty so to do? It is suspected of lukewarmness to suppose it necessary, and a tendency to apostacy to go about it. And if a man can bring his mind once to be positive and fierce for positions whose evidence he has never once examined, and that in matters of greatest concernment to him, what shall keep him from this short and easy way of being in the right in cases of less moment? Thus we are taught to clothe our minds as we do our bodies after the fashion in vogue, and it is accounted fantasticalness, or something worse, not to do so. This custom (which who dares oppose?) makes the short-sighted bigots, and the warier sceptics, as far as it prevails. And those that break from it are in danger of heresy; for, taking the whole world, how much of it doth truth and orthodoxy possess together? Though it is by the last alone (which has the good luck to be every where) that error and heresy are judged of; for argument and evidence signify nothing in the case, and excuse no where, but are sure to be borne down in all societies by the infallible orthodoxy of the place. Whether this be the way to truth and right assent, let the opinions, that take place and prescribe in the several habitable parts of the earth, declare. I never saw any reason yet why truth might not be trusted to its own evidence; I am sure, if that be not able to support it, there is no fence against error, and then truth and falsehood are but names that stand for the same things. Evidence therefore is that by which alone every man is (and should be) taught to regulate his assent, who is then and then only in the right way when he follows it.

Men deficient in knowledge, are usually in one of these three states: either wholly ignorant; or as doubting of some proposition they have either embraced formerly, or at present are inclined to; or, lastly, they do with assurance hold and profess, without ever having examined and been convinced by well grounded arguments.

The first of these are in the best state of the three, by having their minds yet in their perfect freedom and indifferency, the likelier to pursue truth the better, having no bias yet clapped on to mislead them.

SECTION XXXV.

IGNORANCE WITH INDIFFERENCY.

For ignorance with an indifferency for truth is nearer to it, than opinion with ungrounded inclination, which is the great source of error; and they are more in danger to go out of the way who are marching under the conduct of a guide, that it is a hundred to one will mislead them, than he that has not yet taken a step and is likelier to be prevailed on to enquire after the right way.

The last of the three sorts are in the worst condition of all; for if a man can be persuaded and
fully assured of any thing for a truth, without having
examined, what is there that he may not embrace
for truth? And if he has given himself up to believe
a lie, what means is there left to recover one who can
be assured without examining? To the other two this
I crave leave to say, that as he that is ignorant is in
the best state of the two, so he should pursue truth in
a method suitable to that state, i.e. by enquiring directly
into the nature of the thing itself, without minding the
opinions of others, or troubling himself with their questions or disputes about it, but to see what he himself can,
sincerely searching after truth, find out. He that proceeds
upon other principles in his enquiry into any sciences,
though he be resolved to examine them and judge of
them freely, does yet at least put himself on that side,
and post himself in a party which he will not quit till he
be beaten out; by which the mind is insensibly engaged
to make what defence it can, and so is unawares biassed.
I do not say but a man should embrace some opinion
when he has examined, else he examines to no purpose;
but the surest and safest way is to have no opinion at all
till he has examined, and that without any the least regard
to the opinions or systems of other men about it. For
example, were it my business to understand physic, would
not the safer and readier way be to consult nature herself,
and inform myself in the history of diseases and their
cures, than espousing the principles of the dogmatists,
methodists, or chymists, engage in all the disputes concerning either of those systems, and suppose it true,
till I have tried what they can say to beat me out of it.
Or, supposing that Hippocrates, or any other book,

infallibly contains the whole art of physic, would not the direct way be to study, read and consider that book, weigh and compare the parts of it to find the truth, rather than espouse the doctrines of any party, who, though they acknowledge his authority, have already interpreted and wiredrawn all his text to their own sense; the tincture whereof when I have imbibed, I am more in danger to misunderstand his true meaning, than if I had come to him with a mind unprepossessed by doctors and commentators of my sect, whose reasonings, interpretation, and language, which I have been used to, will of course make all chime that way, and make another and perhaps the genuine meaning of the author seem harsh, strained, and uncouth to me. For words, having naturally none of their own, carry that signification to the hearer that he is used to put upon them, whatever be the sense of him that uses them. This, I think, is visibly so; and if it be, he that begins to have any doubt of any of his tenets, which he received without examination, ought, as much as he can, to put himself wholly into this state of ignorance in reference to that question, and throwing wholly by all his former notions, and the opinions of others, examine, with a perfect indifferency, the question in its source, without any inclination to either side, or any regard to his or others' unexamined opinions. This I own is no easy thing to do, but I am not enquiring the easy way to opinion, but the right way to truth; which they must follow who will deal fairly with their own understandings and their own souls.

SECTION XXXVI.

QUESTION.

The indifferency that I here propose will also enable them to state the question right, which they are in doubt about, without which they can never come to a fair and clear decision of it.

SECTION XXXVII.

PERSEVERANCE.

Another fruit from this indifferency and the considering things in themselves, abstract from our own opinions and other men's notions and discourses on them, will be that each man will pursue his thoughts in that method which will be most agreeable to the nature of the thing and to his apprehension of what it suggests to him; in which he ought to proceed with regularity and constancy, until he come to a well-grounded resolution wherein he may acquiesce. If it be objected that this will require every man to be a scholar, and quit all his other business, and betake himself wholly to study; I answer, I propose no more to any one than he has time for. Some men's state and condition requires no great extent of knowledge; the necessary provision for life swallows the greatest part of their time. But one man's want of leisure is no excuse for the oscitancy and ignorance of those who have time to spare; and every one has enough to get as much knowledge as is required and expected of him, and he that does not that is in love with ignorance, and is accountable for it.

SECTION XXXVIII.

PRESUMPTION.

The variety of distempers in men's minds is as great as of those in their bodies; some are epidemic, few escape them, and every one too, if he would look into himself, would find some defect of his particular genius. There is scarce any one without some idiosyncrasy that he suffers by. This man presumes upon his parts, that they will not fail him at time of need, and so thinks it superfluous labour to make any provision before hand. His understanding is to him like Fortunatus's purse, which is always to furnish him without ever putting any thing into it before-hand; and so he sits still satisfied, without endeavouring to store his understanding with knowledge. It is the spontaneous product of the country, and what need of labour in tillage? Such men may spread their native riches before the ignorant; but they were best not come to stress and trial with the skilful. We are born ignorant of every thing. The superficies of things that surround them make impressions on the negligent, but no body penetrates into the inside without labour, attention, and industry. Stones and timber grow of themselves, but yet there is no uniform pile with symmetry and convenience to lodge in without toil and pains. God has made the intellectual world harmonious and beautiful without us; but it will never come into our heads all at once; we must bring it home piecemeal, and there set it up by our own industry, or else we shall have nothing but darkness and a chaos within, whatever order and light there be in things without us.

SECTION XXXIX.

DESPONDENCY.

On the other side, there are others that depress their own minds, despond at the first difficulty, and conclude that the getting an insight in any of the sciences or making any progress in knowledge, farther than serves their ordinary business, is above their capacities. These sit still, because they think they have not legs to go; as the others I last mentioned do, because they think they have wings to fly, and can soar on high when they please. To these latter one may for answer apply the proverb, *Use legs and have legs*. No body knows what strength of parts he has till he has tried them. And of the understanding one may most truly say, that its force is greater generally than it thinks, till it is put to it. *Viresque acquirit eundo.*

And therefore the proper remedy here is but to set the mind to work, and apply the thoughts vigorously to the business; for it holds in the struggles of the mind, as in those of war, *Dum putant se vincere, vicere*; a persuasion that we shall overcome any difficulties that we meet with in the sciences seldom fails to carry us through them. No body knows the strength of his mind and the force of steady and regular application, till he has tried. This is certain, he that sets out upon weak legs will not only go farther, but grow stronger too than one who, with a vigorous constitution and firm limbs, only sits still.

Something of kin to this men may observe in themselves, when the mind frights itself (as it often does) with any thing reflected on in gross, and transiently viewed confusedly and at a distance. Things, thus offered to the mind, carry the shew of nothing but difficulty in them, and are thought to be wrapped up in impenetrable obscurity. But the truth is, these are nothing but spectres that the understanding raises to itself to flatter its own laziness. It sees nothing distinctly in things remote and in a huddle, and therefore concludes too faintly that there is nothing more clear to be discovered in them. It is but to approach nearer, and that mist of our own raising that enveloped them will remove; and those that in that mist appeared hideous giants, not to be grappled with, will be found to be of the ordinary and natural size and shape. Things that in a remote and confused view seem very obscure, must be approached by gentle and regular steps; and what is most visible, easy, and obvious in them first considered. Reduce them into their distinct parts; and then, in their due order, bring all that should be known concerning every one of those parts into plain and simple questions; and then what was thought obscure, perplexed, and too hard for our weak parts, will lay itself open to the understanding in a fair view, and let the mind into that which before it was awed with and kept at a distance from, as wholly mysterious. I appeal to my reader's experience, whether this has never happened to him, especially when, busy on one thing, he has occasionally reflected on another. I ask him, whether he has never thus been scared with a sudden opinion of mighty difficulties, which yet have vanished, when he has seriously and methodically applied himself to the consideration of this seeming terrible subject; and there has been no other matter of astonishment left, but that he amused himself with so discouraging a prospect of his own rais-

ing about a matter which, in the handling, was found to
have nothing in it more strange nor intricate than several
other things which he had long since and with ease mastered? This experience should teach us how to deal with
such bugbears another time, which should rather serve to
excite our vigour than enervate our industry. The surest
way for a learner, in this as in all other cases, is not to
advance by jumps and large strides; let that which he
sets himself to learn next be indeed the next, i. e. as
nearly conjoined with what he knows already as is possible; let it be distinct but not remote from it: let it
be new and what he did not know before, that the
understanding may advance ; but let it be as little at
once as may be, that its advances may be clear and sure.
All the ground that it gets this way it will hold. This
distinct gradual growth in knowledge is firm and sure,
it carries its own light with it in every step of its progression in an easy and orderly train, than which there is
nothing of more use to the understanding. And though
this perhaps may seem a very slow and lingering way to
knowledge, yet I dare confidently affirm that whoever will
try it in himself, or any one he will teach, shall find the
advances greater in this method than they would. in the
same space of time, have been in any other he could have
taken. The greatest part of true knowledge lies in a
distinct perception of things in themselves distinct. And
some men give more clear light and knowledge by the
bare distinct stating of a question, than others by talking
of it in gross whole hours together. In this, they who
so state a question do no more but separate and disen-
tangle the parts of it one from another, and lay them,
when so disentangled, in their due order. This often, ·
without any more ado, resolves the doubt, and shews

the mind where the truth lies. The agreement or disagreement of the ideas in question, when they are once separated and distinctly considered, is, in many cases, presently perceived, and thereby clear and lasting knowledge gained; whereas things in gross taken up together, and so lying together in confusion, can produce in the mind but a confused, which in effect is no knowledge, or at least, when it comes to be examined and made use of, will prove little better than none. I therefore take the liberty to repeat here again what I have said elsewhere, that, in learning any thing, as little should be proposed to the mind at once as is possible; and, that being understood and fully mastered, to proceed to the next adjoining part yet unknown, simple, unperplexed proposition belonging to the matter in hand, and tending to the clearing what is principally designed.

SECTION XL.

ANALOGY.

Analogy is of great use to the mind in many cases, especially in natural philosophy, and that part of it chiefly which consists in happy and successful experiments. But here we must take care that we keep ourselves within that wherein the analogy consists. For example, the acid oil of vitriol is found to be good in such a case, therefore the spirit of nitre or vinegar may be used in the like case. If the good effect of it be owing wholly to the acidity of it, the trial may be justified; but if there be something else besides the acidity in the oil of vitriol, which produces the good we desire in the case, we mistake that for analogy, which is not, and suffer our understanding to be misguided by a wrong supposition of analogy where there is none.

SECTION XLI.

ASSOCIATION.

Though I have, in the second book of my Essay concerning Human Understanding, treated of the association of ideas; yet having done it there historically, as giving a view of the understanding in this as well as its several other ways of operating, rather than designing there to enquire into the remedies [that] ought to be applied to it: it will, under this latter consideration, afford other matter of thought to those who have a mind to instruct themselves thoroughly in the right way of conducting their understandings; and that the rather, because this, if I mistake not, is as frequent a cause of mistake and error in us as perhaps any thing else that can be named, and is a disease of the mind as hard to be cured as any; it being a very hard thing to convince any one that things are not so, and naturally so, as they constantly appear to him.

By this one easy and unheeded miscarriage of the understanding, sandy and loose foundations become infallible principles, and will not suffer themselves to be touched or questioned: such unnatural connections become by custom as natural to the mind, as sun and light. Fire and warmth go together, and so seem to carry with them as natural an evidence as self-evident truths themselves. And where then shall one with hopes of success begin the cure? Many men firmly embrace falsehood for truth; not only because they never thought otherwise, but also because, thus blinded as they have been from the beginning, they never could think otherwise; at least without a vigour of mind able to contest the empire of habit, and look into its own principles, a freedom which few men have the notion of in themselves, and fewer are allowed the practice of by others; it being the great art and business of the teachers and guides in most sects, to suppress, as much as they can, this fundamental duty which every man owes himself, and [which] is the first steady step towards right and truth in the whole train of his actions and opinions. This would give one reason to suspect that such teachers are conscious to themselves of the falsehood or weakness of the tenets they profess, since they will not suffer the grounds whereon they are built to be examined; whereas those who seek truth only, and desire to own and propagate nothing else, freely expose their principles to the test, are pleased to have them examined, give men leave to reject them if they can, and, if there be any thing weak and unsound in them, are willing to have it detected, that they themselves, as well as others, may not lay any stress upon any received proposition beyond what the evidence of its truth will warrant and allow.

There is, I know, a great fault among all sorts of people of principling their children and scholars; which at last, when looked into, amounts to no more but making them imbibe their teachers' notions and tenets by an implicit faith, and firmly to adhere to them whether true or false. What colours may be given to this, or of what use it may be when practised upon the vulgar, destined to labour and given up to the service of their bellies, I will not here enquire. But as to the ingenuous part of mankind, whose condition allows them leisure, and letters, and enquiry after truth, I can see no other right way of principling them, but to take heed, as much as may be, that, in their tender years, ideas that have no natural cohesion come not to be united in their heads, and that this rule be often inculcated to them to be their guide in the whole course of their lives and studies, viz. that they never suffer any ideas to be joined in their understandings in any other or stronger combination than what their own nature and correspondence give them; and that they often examine those that they find linked together in their minds, whether this association of ideas be from the visible agreement that is in the ideas themselves, or from the habitual and prevailing custom of the mind joining them thus together in thinking.

This is for caution against this evil, before it be thoroughly riveted by custom in the understanding; but he that would cure it, when habit has established it, must nicely observe the very quick and almost imperceptible motions of the mind in its habitual actions. What I have said in another place about the change of the ideas of sense into those of judgment may be proof of this. Let any one not skilled in painting be told when he sees bottles and tobacco pipes, and other things so painted, as they are in some places shewn, that he does not see protuberances, and you will not convince him but by the touch: he will not believe that, by an instantaneous legerdemain of his own thoughts, one idea is substituted for the other. How frequent instances may one meet with of this in the arguings of the learned, who not seldom, in two ideas that they have been accustomed to join in their minds, substitute one for the other; and, I am apt to think, often without perceiving it themselves. This, whilst they are under the deceit of it, makes them incapable of conviction, and they applaud themselves as zealous champions for truth, when indeed they are contending for error. And the confusion of two different ideas, which a customary connection of them in their minds hath made to them almost one, fills their heads with false views, and their reasonings with false consequences.

SECTION XLII.

FALLACIES.

Right understanding consists in the discovery and adherence to truth, and that in the perception of the visible or probable agreement or disagreement of ideas, as they are affirmed and denied one of another. From whence it is evident that the right use and conduct of the understanding, whose business is purely truth and nothing else, is that the mind should be kept in a perfect indifferency, not inclining to either side, any farther than evidence settles it by knowledge, or the overbalance of probability gives it the turn of assent and belief; but yet it is very hard to meet with any discourse, wherein one may not perceive the author not only maintain (for that is reasonable and fit) but inclined and biassed to one side of the question, with marks of a desire that that should be true. If it be asked me, how authors who have such a bias and lean to it may be discovered, I answer, by observing how, in their writings or arguings, they are often led by their inclinations to change the ideas of the question, either by changing the terms, or by adding and joining others to them, whereby the ideas under consideration are so varied as to be more serviceable to their purpose, and to be thereby brought to an easier and nearer agreement or more visible and remoter disagreement one with another. This is plain and direct sophistry; but I am far from thinking that, wherever it is found, it is made use of with design to deceive and mislead the readers. It is visible that men's prejudices and inclinations by this way impose often upon themselves; and their affections for truth, under their prepossession in favour of one side, is the very thing that leads them from it. Inclination suggests and slides into their discourse favourable terms, which introduce favourable ideas, till at last, by this means, that is concluded clear and evident, thus dressed up, which taken in its native state, by making use of none but the precise determined ideas, would find no admittance at all. The putting these glosses on what they affirm, these, as they are thought, handsome, easy, and graceful explications of what they are discoursing on, is so much the character of what is called and esteemed writing well, that it is very hard to think that authors will ever be persuaded to leave what serves so well to propagate their opinions and procure themselves credit in the world, for a more jejune and dry way of writing, by keeping to the same terms precisely annexed to the same ideas, a sour and blunt stiffness tolerable in mathematicians only, who force their way and make truth prevail by irresistible demonstration.

But yet if authors cannot be prevailed with to quit the looser, though more insinuating, ways of writing, if they will not think fit to keep close to truth and instruction by unvaried terms and plain unsophisticated arguments, yet it concerns readers not to be imposed on by fallacies and the prevailing ways of insinuation. To do this, the surest and most effectual remedy is to fix in the mind the clear and distinct ideas of the question stripped of words; and so likewise, in the train of argumentation, to take up the author's ideas, neglecting his words, observing how they connect or separate those in the question. He that does this will be able to cast off all that is superfluous; he will see what is pertinent, what coherent, what is direct to, what slides by the question. This will readily shew him all the foreign ideas in the discourse, and where they were brought in; and though they perhaps dazzled the writer, yet he will perceive that they give no light nor strength to his reasonings.

This, though it be the shortest and easiest way of reading books with profit, and keeping one's self from being misled by great names or plausible discourses, yet, it being hard and tedious to those who have not accustomed themselves to it, it is not to be expected that every one (amongst those few who really pursue truth) should this way guard his understanding from being imposed on by the wilful or, at least, undesigned sophistry, which creeps into most of the books of argument. They that write against their conviction, or that next to them are resolved to maintain the tenets of a party they are engaged in, cannot be supposed to reject any arms that may help to defend their cause, and therefore such should be read with the greatest caution. And they who write for opinions they are sincerely persuaded of, and believe to be true, think they may so far allow themselves to indulge their laudable affection to truth, as to permit their esteem of it to give it the best colours, and set it off with the best expressions and dress they can, thereby to gain it the easiest entrance into the minds of their readers and fix it deepest there.

One of those being the state of mind we may justly

suppose most writers to be in, it is fit their readers, who apply to them for instruction, should not lay by that caution which becomes a sincere pursuit of truth and should make them always watchful against whatever might conceal or misrepresent it. If they have not the skill of representing to themselves the author's sense by pure ideas separated from sounds, and thereby divested of the false lights and deceitful ornaments of speech, this yet they should do, they should keep the precise question steadily in their minds, carry it along with them through the whole discourse, and suffer not the least alteration in the terms, either by addition, subtraction, or substituting any other. This every one can do who has a mind to it: and he that has not a mind to it, it is plain makes his understanding only the warehouse of other men's lumber; I mean, false and unconcluding reasonings, rather than a repository of truth for his own use, which will prove substantial and stand him in stead when he has occasion for it. And whether such an one deals fairly by his own mind, and conducts his own understanding right, I leave to his own understanding to judge.

SECTION XLIII.

FUNDAMENTAL VERITIES.

The mind of man being very narrow, and so slow in making acquaintance with things and taking in new truths that no one man is capable, in a much longer life than ours, to know all truths; it becomes our prudence, in our search after knowledge, to employ our thoughts about fundamental and material questions, carefully avoiding those that are trifling, and not suffering ourselves to be diverted from our main even purpose by those that are merely incidental. How much of many young men's time is thrown away in purely logical enquiries, I need not mention. This is no better than if a man, who was to be a painter, should spend all his time in examining the threads of the several cloths he is to paint upon, and counting the hairs of each pencil and brush he intends to use in the laying on of his colours. Nay, it is much worse than for a young painter to spend his apprenticeship in such useless niceties; for he, at the end of all his pains to no purpose, finds that it is not painting, nor any help to it, and so is really to no purpose. Whereas men designed for scholars have often their heads so filled and warmed with disputes on logical questions, that they take those airy useless notions for real and substantial knowledge, and think their understandings so well furnished with science that they need not look any farther into the nature of things, or descend to the mechanical drudgery of experiment and inquiry. This is so obvious a mismanagement of the understanding, and that in the professed way to knowledge, that it could not be passed by; to which might be joined abundance of questions, and the way of handling of them in the schools. What faults in particular of this kind every man is, or may be guilty of, would be infinite to enumerate; it suffices to have shewn that superficial and slight discoveries and observations that contain nothing of moment in themselves, nor serve as clues to lead us into farther knowledge, should be lightly passed by, and never thought worth our searching after. There are fundamental truths that lie at the bottom, the basis upon which a great many others rest, and in which they have their consistency. These are teeming truths, rich in

store, with which they furnish the mind, and, like the
lights of heaven, are not only beautiful and entertaining
in themselves, but give light and evidence to other things
that without them could not be seen or known. Such is
that admirable discovery of Mr. Newton, that all bodies
gravitate to one another, which may be counted as the
basis of natural philosophy; which of what use it is
to the understanding of the great frame of our solar
system, he has to the astonishment of the learned world
shewn, and how much farther it would guide us in other
things, if rightly pursued, is not yet known. Our
Saviour's great rule, that *we should love our neighbour as
ourselves*, is such a fundamental truth for the regulating
human society, that I think by that alone one might
without difficulty determine all the cases and doubts in
social morality. These, and such as these, are the truths
we should endeavour to find out and store our minds
with. Which leads me to another thing in the conduct
of the understanding that is no less necessary, viz.

SECTION XLIV.

BOTTOMING.

To accustom ourselves in any question proposed to
examine and find out upon what it bottoms. Most of
the difficulties that come in our way, when well considered
and traced, lead us to some proposition which, known to
be true, clears the doubt, and gives an easy solution of
the question, whilst topical and superficial arguments,
of which there is store to be found on both sides, filling
the head with variety of thoughts and the mouth with
copious discourse, serve only to amuse the understanding,

and entertain company, without coming to the bottom of the question, the only place of rest and stability for an inquisitive mind whose tendency is only to truth and knowledge.

For example, if it be demanded, whether the grand seignior can lawfully take what he will from any of his people? This question cannot be resolved without coming to a certainty, whether all men are naturally equal; for upon that it turns, and that truth, well settled in the understanding and carried in the mind through the various debates concerning the various rights of men in society, will go a great way in putting an end to them and shewing on which side the truth is.

SECTION XLV.

TRANSFERRING OF THOUGHTS.

There is scarce any thing more for the improvement of knowledge, for the ease of life, and the dispatch of business, than for a man to be able to dispose of his own thoughts; and there is scarce anything harder in the whole conduct of the understanding, than to get a full mastery over it. The mind, in a waking man, has always some object that it applies itself to; which, when we are lazy or unconcerned, we can easily change, and at pleasure transfer our thoughts to another, and from thence to a third, which has no relation to either of the former. Hence men forwardly conclude, and frequently say, nothing is so free as thought, and it were well it were so; but the contrary will be found true in several instances; and there are many cases wherein there is nothing more resty and ungovernable than our thoughts: they will not be directed what objects to pursue, nor be taken off from those they have once fixed on, but run away with a man in pursuit of those ideas they have in view, let him do what he can.

I will not here mention again what I have above taken notice of, how hard it is to get the mind, narrowed by a custom of thirty or forty years standing to a scanty collection of obvious and common ideas, to enlarge itself to a more copious stock, and grow into an acquaintance with those that would afford more abundant matter of useful contemplation; it is not of this I am here speaking. The inconvenience I would here represent and find a remedy for, is the difficulty there is sometimes to transfer our minds from one subject to another, in cases where the ideas are equally familiar to us.

Matters that are recommended to our thoughts by any of our passions take possession of our minds with a kind of authority, and will not be kept out or dislodged, but, as if the passion that rules were, for the time, the sheriff of the place, and came with all the posse, the understanding is seized and taken with the object it introduces, as if it had a legal right to be alone considered there. There is scarce any body, I think, of so calm a temper who hath not sometime found this tyranny on his understanding, and suffered under the inconvenience of it. Who is there almost whose mind, at some time or other, love or anger, fear or grief, has not so fastened to some clog, that it could not turn itself to any other object? I call it a clog, for it hangs upon the mind so as to hinder its vigour and activity in the pursuit of other contemplations, and advances itself little or not [at] all in the knowledge of the thing which it so closely hugs and constantly pores on.

Men thus possessed are sometimes as if they were so in the worst sense, and lay under the power of an enchantment. They see not what passes before their eyes; hear not the audible discourse of the company; and when by any strong application to them they are roused a little, they are like men brought to themselves from some remote region; whereas in truth they come no farther than their secret cabinet within, where they have been wholly taken up with the puppet, which is for that time appointed for their entertainment. The shame that such dumps cause to well-bred people, when it carries them away from the company, where they should bear a part in the conversation, is a sufficient argument that it is a fault in the conduct of our understanding, not to have that power over it as to make use of it to those purposes and on those occasions wherein we have need of its assistance. The mind should be always free and ready to turn itself to the variety of objects that occur, and allow them as much consideration as shall for that time be thought fit. To be engrossed so by one object, as not to be prevailed on to leave it for another that we judge fitter for our contemplation, is to make it of no use to us. Did this state of mind remain always so, every one would, without scruple, give it the name of perfect madness; and whilst it does last, at whatever intervals it returns, such a rotation of thoughts about the same object no more carries us forwards towards the attainment of knowledge, than getting upon a mill-horse whilst he jogs on in his circular track would carry a man a journey.

I grant something must be allowed to legitimate passions and to natural inclinations. Every man, besides occasional affections, has beloved studies, and those the mind will more closely stick to; but yet it is best that it should be always at liberty, and under the free disposal of the man, to act how and upon what he directs. This we should endeavour to obtain, unless we would be content with such a flaw in our understandings, that sometimes we should be as it were without it; for it is very little better than so in cases where we cannot make use of it to those purposes we would and which stand in present need of it.

But before fit remedies can be thought on for this disease, we must know the several causes of it, and thereby regulate the cure, if we will hope to labour with success.

One we have already instanced in, whereof all men that reflect have so general a knowledge, and so often an experience in themselves, that no body doubts of it. A prevailing passion so pins down our thoughts to the object and concern of it, that a man passionately in love cannot bring himself to think of his ordinary affairs, or a kind mother, drooping under the loss of a child, is not able to bear a part as she was wont in the discourse of the company or conversation of her friends.

But though passion be the most obvious and general, yet it is not the only cause that binds up the understanding, and confines it for the time to one object from which it will not be taken off.

Besides this, we may often find that the understanding, when it has a while employed itself upon a subject which either chance, or some slight accident, offered to it without the interest or recommendation of any passion, works itself into a warmth, and by degrees gets into a career, wherein, like a bowl down a hill, it increases its motion by going, and will not be stopped or diverted, though, when the heat is over, it sees all this earnest application was about a trifle not worth a thought, and all the pains employed about it lost labour.

There is a third sort, if I mistake not, yet lower than this; it is a sort of childishness, if I may so say, of the understanding, wherein, during the fit, it plays with and dandles some insignificant puppet to no end, nor with any design at all, and yet cannot easily be got off from it. Thus some trivial sentence, or a scrap of poetry, will sometimes get into men's heads, and make such a chiming there, that there is no stilling of it; no peace to be obtained, nor attention to any thing else, but this impertinent guest will take up the mind and possess the thoughts in spite of all endeavours to get rid of it. Whether every one hath experimented in themselves this troublesome intrusion of some striking ideas which thus importune the understanding, and hinder it from being better employed, I know not. But persons of very good parts, and those more than one, I have heard speak and complain of it themselves. The reason I have to make this doubt is from what I have known in a case something of kin to this, though much odder, and that is of a sort of visions that some people have lying quiet but perfectly awake in the dark, or with their eyes shut. It is a great variety of faces, most commonly very odd ones, that appear to them in a train one after another; so that having had just the sight of one, it immediately passes away to give place to another that the same instant succeeds and has as quick an exit as its leader, and so they march on in a constant succession; nor can any one of them by any endeavour be stopped or retained beyond the instant of its appearance, but is thrust out by its follower, which will have its turn. Concerning this fantastical phenomenon I have talked with several people, whereof some have been perfectly acquainted with it, and others have been so wholly strangers to it, that they could hardly be brought to conceive or believe it. I knew a lady of excellent parts, who had got past thirty without having ever had the least notice of any such thing ; she was so great a stranger to it that, when she heard me and another talking of it, [she] could scarce forbear thinking we bantered her ; but sometime after, drinking a large dose of dilute tea (as she was ordered by a physician) going to bed, she told us at next meeting, that she had now experimented what our discourse had much ado to persuade her of. She had seen a great variety of faces in a long train, succeeding one another, as we had described ; they were all strangers and intruders, such as she had no acquaintance with before, nor sought after then, and as they came of themselves they went too ; none of them stayed a moment, nor could be detained by all the endeavours she could use, but went on in their solemn procession, just appeared and then vanished. This odd phenomenon seems to have a mechanical cause, and to depend upon the matter and motion of the blood or animal spirits.

When the fancy is bound by passion, I know no way to set the mind free and at liberty to prosecute what thoughts the man would make choice of, but to allay the present passion, or counterbalance it with another, which is an art to be got by study and acquaintance with the passions.

Those who find themselves apt to be carried away with the spontaneous current of their own thoughts, not excited by any passion or interest, must be very wary and careful in all the instances of it to stop it, and never humour their minds in being thus triflingly busy. Men know the value of their corporal liberty, and therefore suffer not willingly fetters and chains to be put upon them. To have the mind captivated is, for the time, certainly the greater evil of the two, and deserves our utmost care and endeavours to preserve the freedom of our better part. And in this case our pains will not be lost; striving and struggling will prevail, if we constantly, in all such occasions, make use of it. We must never indulge these trivial attentions of thought; as soon as we find the mind makes itself a business of nothing, we should immediately disturb and check it, introduce new and more serious considerations, and not leave till we have beaten it off from the pursuit it was upon. This, at first, if we have let the contrary practice grow to a habit, will perhaps be difficult; but constant endeavours will by degrees prevail, and at last make it easy. And when a man is pretty well advanced, and can command his mind off at pleasure from incidental and undesigned pursuits, it may not be amiss for him to go on farther, and make attempts upon meditations of greater moment, that at the last he may have a full power over his own mind, and be so fully master of his own thoughts, as to be able to transfer them from one subject to another with the same ease that he can lay by any thing he has in his hand and take something else that he has a mind to in the room of it. This liberty of mind is of great use both in business and study, and he that has got it will have no small advantage of ease and despatch in all that is the chosen and useful employment of his understanding.

The third and last way which I mentioned the mind to be sometimes taken up with, I mean the chiming of some particular words or sentence in the memory, and, as it were, making a noise in the head, and the like, seldom happens but when the mind is lazy or very loosely and negligently employed. It were better indeed be without such impertinent and useless repetitions; any obvious idea, when it is roving causelessly at a venture, being of more use and apter to suggest something worth consideration, than the insignificant buzz of purely empty sounds. But since the rousing of the mind, and setting the understanding on work with some degrees of vigour, does for the most part presently set it free from these idle companions; it may not be amiss, whenever we find ourselves troubled with them, to make use of so profitable a remedy that is always at hand.

NOTES.

SECTION I.

Page 3. *operative powers are directed.* Cp. Essay on the Human Understanding, Bk. II, ch. 21, § 29: ' The Will is nothing but a power in the Mind to direct the operative faculties of a man to motion or rest. To the question, What is it determines the Will? the true and proper answer is, The Mind. For that which determines the general power of directing to this or that particular direction, is nothing but the agent itself exercising the power it has that particular way. If this answer satisfies not, 'tis plain the meaning of the question, What determines the Will? is this, What moves the Mind, in every particular instance, to determine its general power of directing to this or that particular motion or rest? And to this I answer, The motive for continuing in the same state or action, is only the present Satisfaction in it : the motive to change is always some Uneasiness ; nothing setting us upon the change of state, or upon any new action, but some Uneasiness. This is the great motive that works on the Mind to put it upon action, which for shortness sake we will call determining of the Will.' Locke's theory of volition seems, in brief, to be this : something, suggested by desire in the first instance, is, on reflection, regarded by the understanding as desirable ; this motive, as it may be called, produces uneasiness ; the uneasiness determines the will, and the will, thus directed, results in action.

Page 4. *two or three thousand years.* The date of Aristotle, from whom the scholastic logic was, with certain additions and modifications, derived, is the fourth century before Christ. He was born not earlier than 392 B.C., nor later than 384 B.C. He died in 322 B.C. But many traces of his logical doctrine are already to be found in Plato, and some may be carried back even as far as Zeno the Eleatic, who is said to have been born about 488 B.C.

Lord Verulam's, that is, Francis Bacon, b. 1560-1, d. 1626, who was created Baron Verulam, and subsequently Viscount St. Alban. He is commonly, but inaccurately, called Lord Bacon.

preface to his Novum Organum.   This passage is to be found, not in the preface to the Novum Organum, but in that to the Instauratio Magna generally, of which great, but unfinished, undertaking the Novum Organum was designed to be the second part. This preface, with other small pieces, was, however, published along with the Novum Organum. The sentences quoted will be found in my edition of the Novum Organum, 2nd ed. p. 165, or in Ellis and Spedding's Edition, vol. i, p. 129.

but became a part of it, literally, 'nor is it without evil itself.'

which took place, literally, 'which is received,' that is, which is in common use.

subtilty.   This, or subtility, is the old way of spelling subtlety, which is derived from the Latin word *subtilitas.*

SECTION III.

Page 8. *of one sort of notions.*   Cp. Bacon, Novum Organum, Bk. i, Aph. 54: 'Adamant homines scientias et contemplationes particulares ; aut quia auctores et inventores se earum credunt ; aut quia plurimum in illis operae posuerunt, iisque maxime assueverunt. Hujusmodi vero homines, si ad philosophiam et contemplationes universales se contulerint, illas ex prioribus phantasiis detorquent et corrumpunt.' He then goes on to exemplify this 'idol of the den' in Aristotle, 'qui naturalem suam philosophiam logicae suae prorsus mancipavit,' in the Alchemists, and in Gilbert, who is charged with having subordinated the whole of his system to magnetism.

Marian Islands.   Properly the Marianne or Ladrone Islands. These, to the number of about twenty, lie in the North Pacific Ocean, between the 13th and 21st degrees of N. lat. and the 144th and 146th of E. long.   They were originally discovered in 1521, by Magellan, who called them Las Islas de los Ladrones, or the Isles of Thieves, on account of the thievish propensities of their inhabitants.   They were subsequently called the Mariana or Marianne Islands from Mary Ann of Austria, queen of Spain, at whose expense Christian missionaries were sent over for their conversion. The statements made by Locke will be found in Martinière's Dictionnaire Géographique et Critique.   When Magellan set fire, as a punishment, to some of their huts and trees, the islanders are said to have taken the fire for an animal, devouring its prey.

Page 9. *hold fast that which is good.* 1 Thess. v. 21. In the English Version '*prove* all things.' The Greek word is δοκιμάζετε. The Apostle does not use these expressions in the same general sense as that in which Locke applies them, but is referring specially to χαρίσματα, spiritual gifts, real or assumed.

hid treasure. See Proverbs ii. 4.

Page 11. *errant.* This word is used here in the sense of 'arrant' = thorough, and probably confounded with it. Mr. Skeat (Etymological Dictionary of the English Language) has pointed out that the two words 'errant' and 'arrant,' though generally supposed to be merely different modes of spelling the same word, are of entirely different origin. 'Errant' = wandering, as in the expression 'knight-errant,' is of French origin; 'arrant' is a corruption of *arghand,* the Northumbrian present participle of the Northern English verb 'argh' = to fear. It is closely connected with 'arch,' and its earlier meanings are 'fearing,' 'cowardly,' 'knavish.'

SECTION IV.

Page 14. *to their perfection.* This is a very common topic with moralists and psychologists. The readers of Aristotle will be reminded of several places in Eth. Nic. Bk. II, especially ch. 1.

Page 15. *wherein right reasoning consists.* Both here and in the Thoughts concerning Education, Locke undoubtedly undervalues the importance of rhetorical and logical rules, as offering guidance for effective speaking or correct reasoning, and contributing to protect the mind from the influence of sophisms. The passage (§ 188) in the Thoughts concerning Education may be compared with that in the text. 'Rhetoric and Logic, being the arts that in the ordinary method usually follow immediately after grammar, it may perhaps be wondered that I have said so little of them. The reason is, because of the little advantage young people receive by them. For I have seldom or never observed any one to get the skill of reasoning well or speaking handsomely, by studying those rules which pretend to teach it. And therefore I would have a young gentleman take a view of them in the shortest systems could be found, without dwelling long on the contemplation and study of those formalities. Right Reasoning is founded on something else than the

Predicaments and Predicables, and does not consist in talking in Mode and Figure itself. But it is besides my present business to enlarge upon this speculation. To come therefore to what we have in hand : if you would have your son reason well, let him read Chillingworth ; and if you would have him speak well, let him be conversant in Tully, to give him the true idea of eloquence ; and let him read those things that are well writ in English, to perfect his style in the purity of our language.'

To teach children or youths a number of mere abstract rules, without constant application and illustration, is the most senseless mode of education that could be devised. And it will always be a question whether, instead of beginning with the rule, we ought not to begin with the concrete instance, and, by analysis of the sentence or argument, shew the meaning or establish the validity of the rule. Thus, to listen to the best speakers may be the best way of learning to speak with effect ; to read the best writers of learning to write in a clear, forcible, and interesting manner ; to follow, through its various connections, a complicated piece of reasoning the surest method of learning to discriminate between true and false arguments. But, in all these cases, the principles which underlie the art of the successful speaker or the demonstrations of the convincing reasoner ought to be pointed out to the pupil. Wherever we begin, the abstract rule and the concrete illustration ought never to be divorced in the practical work of teaching.

The question of the desirability or utility of teaching rules of rhetoric differs widely from the same question, when considered in reference to logic. So far as the rules of rhetoric aim at mere persuasion, apart from lucid order, agreeable utterance and the like, they may be regarded as devices for enabling a speaker, by manipulating arguments and exciting the passions and affections, to convince his auditors irrespectively of the soundness of the reasoning. But the sole object of the rules of logic is, or ought to be, to preserve the student from imposing by false reasoning upon himself, and to enable him to detect the fallacious reasonings of others. Hence, while the aim of logic is always a desirable one, that of rhetoric is often very questionable. Moreover, when the various rhetorical devices for setting off or detracting from the just force of an argument have once become known to the reader or auditor, he is put on his guard and they cease to have the designed effect ; whereas the observance of the rules of logic is to the common interest of all persons, whether speakers or auditors, writers or readers, whose object is the ascertainment of truth and the avoidance of error.

The reader who wishes to see a defence of logical rules against the attacks of Locke and others may consult Mill's Logic, Introduction, §§ 5, 6, and Bk. III, ch. 9, § 3; also my Inductive Logic, Ch. 3, Appended Note 3. I venture to quote some sentences from the latter work. 'The reply,' whether to those who, like Locke, question the utility of syllogistic rules and formulæ, or to those who, like Whewell, object to formulating any canons in inductive reasoning, is 'that Logic does not profess to *supply* arguments, but to *test* them. Men have certainly reasoned, and reasoned with the greatest force, without any conscious use of the rules of Logic. But it is the province of a system of Logic to analyse the arguments commonly employed, to discriminate between those which are correct and those which are incorrect, and thus to enable men to detect, in the case of others, and to avoid, in their own case, erroneous methods of reasoning. To think of appropriate arguments is undoubtedly more difficult than to test them; but this does not obviate the necessity of submitting them to a test. Nor is it a more real objection that men, who know nothing of the technical rules of Logic, often reason faultlessly themselves, and show remarkable acuteness in detecting inconclusive reasoning in the arguments of others. Many men speak grammatically without having learnt any system of grammar; in the same manner, many men reason logically without having learnt any system of Logic. But the great majority of men, there can be little doubt, may derive assistance both from the one and the other. Grammar fulfils its functions when it raises the student to the level of the most correct speakers; similarly, Logic fulfils its functions when it raises the student to the level of the best reasoners.'

The thorny, wearisome, and often utterly unpractical character of the old logical discipline might well suggest to Locke his objections to it, though these objections do not seem to have gone to the extent of proposing to abolish it altogether. Not only were the examples generally alien to the reasonings of practical life, but a most disproportionate share of the text-books, as well as of the oral instruction, was devoted to topics like the predicaments, post-predicables, predicables, &c., which, if forming any part of Logic

at all, have little direct bearing on its main function. That function
I take to be the examination of evidence, or, in other words, the discrimination of true from false reasoning.

Locke's celebrated attack on the Syllogism is to be found in the
Essay, Bk. IV, ch. 17, §§ 4–6. It is there that he makes the often-
quoted, though irrelevant, remark, that 'God has not been so sparing
to men, to make them barely two-legged creatures, and left it to
Aristotle to make them rational.'

SECTION V.

clear and determined ideas. There is a chapter in the Essay
(Bk. II, ch. 29) entitled 'On Clear and Distinct, Obscure and Confused Ideas.' In § 4 of that chapter, the difference between the
expression 'a *clear* idea' and 'a *distinct* idea' is stated as follows:
'As a *clear idea* is that whereof the mind has such a full and evident
perception as it does receive from an outward object operating duly
on a well-disposed organ, so a *distinct idea* is that wherein the mind
perceives a difference from all other; and a *confused idea* is such an
one, as is not sufficiently distinguishable from another from which
it ought to be different.' Cp. Descartes, Principia, Pt. I, § 45:
'Quin et permulti homines nihil plane in tota vita percipiunt satis
recte, ad certum de eo judicium ferendum. Etenim ad perceptionem
cui certum et indubitatum judicium possit inniti, non modo requiritur
ut sit clara, sed etiam ut sit distincta. Claram voco illam, quae
menti attendenti praesens et aperta est; sicut ea clare a nobis videri
dicimus quae, oculo intuenti praesentia, satis fortiter et aperte illum
movent. Distinctam autem illam, quae, cum clara sit, ab omnibus
aliis ita sejuncta est et praecisa, ut nihil plane aliud quam quod
clarum est in se contineat.' See also Port Royal Logic, Pt. I, ch. 9,
and Leibnitz, Meditationes de Cognitione, Veritate, et Ideis, ad init.
(ed. Erdmann, p. 79). As the terms are discriminated by these authors,
an idea is *clear* so far as we are able to distinguish the various attri-
butes which it implies, *distinct* so far as we are able to distinguish
it, as a whole, from all other ideas. An idea ought, of course, to be
both clear and distinct.

In the Fourth Edition of the Essay, Locke proposed to substitute
for the expression 'clear and distinct' the word 'determined' or
'determinate.' He explains his meaning, in the Epistle to the
Reader, thus: 'By *determinate*, when applied to a *simple idea*, I

mean that simple appearance which the mind has in its view, or perceives in itself, when that idea is said to be in it. By *determined*, when applied to a complex idea, I mean such an one as consists of a determinate number of certain simple or less complex ideas, joined in such a proportion and situation as the mind has before its view and sees in itself when that idea is present in it, or should be present in it when a man gives a name to it. I say *should* be; because it is not every one, nor perhaps any one, who is so careful of his language as to use no word, till he views in his mind the precise determined idea which he resolves to make it the sign of.' To the 'determined idea' a particular sign should be steadily annexed, or, in other words, a name should be *determined* to that precise idea. What Locke seems to mean is that we should always envisage, realise, or explore our ideas, and then take care invariably to employ the same term for the same idea.

Probably he here uses the words 'clear' and 'determined' as synonymous, as he seems to use the words 'clear and determinate,' 'clear and distinct,' in the Essay, Bk. II, ch. 11, § 3. If the terms, however, in this place are meant to be distinguished, 'determined' must be taken as the equivalent of distinct.

in another place. See the whole of the Third Book of the Essay but especially chs. 9, 10, 11. The student, who reads these chapters, will do well to compare Bacon's Novum Organum, Bk. I, Aphorisms 43, 59, 60 (on the 'Idola Fori').

SECTION VI.

Page 16. *principles.* Principia, ἀρχαί, the ultimate major premisses from which our reasonings proceed. These, according to Locke, arise from the laying together and perceiving the agreement of our ideas, and our ideas are all derived from experience, either of the operations of our own minds or of the external world, that is, to use the phraseology of the Essay, either from Sensation or Reflection. See Bk. I, and Bk II, ch. 1. Hence there are no innate principles, inasmuch as there are no innate ideas. To maintain that there are innate principles is 'to take men from the use of their own reason and judgment, and put them upon believing and taking principles upon trust, without further examination : in which posture of blind credulity, men may be more easily governed by, and made useful to, some sort of men, who have the skill and office to principle and guide them.' Bk. I, ch. 4, § 24. Instances of legitimate 'First Principles' are such as these : 'Things that are equal to the same thing are equal to one another'; 'A body under the action of no external force will remain at rest or move uniformly in a straight line' (First Law of Motion); 'The angles of incidence and reflexion of a ray of light are equal'; 'The supply and demand of commodities have a constant tendency to become equalised.' Instances of false 'First Principles' would be such as the circular motion of the planets, the immutability of the heavenly bodies, the decuple proportion, in respect to density and rarity, of the elements, the proposition that the wealth of a country depends upon the excess of its exports over its imports, and the like. All legitimate 'first principles' must either be self-evident or based on careful induction, and even those which appear to be self-evident will be found, on a more exact analysis, to have been originally formed by early and constant inductions. This is alike the doctrine of Bacon and Aristotle. See Aristotle, Anal. Post. II. 19, Metaph. I. 1, Eth. Nic. VI. 3 (3), and Bacon's Novum Organum, Bk. I, Aphs. 13, 14, 19, 105, &c., &c.

embraced for their sake. It is plain that the premises ought to be more certain, at least to the person who employs them, than the conclusion; else they afford no proof. On this fact Aristotle insists in Anal. Post. I. 2.

no ground for. Bacon is never weary of insisting on the necessity of examining first principles, and of condemning the slovenly and indolent manner in which the men of his time were accustomed to accept them either on trust, or on little or no enquiry. See, for instance, Nov. Org. Bk. I, Aphs. 14, 17 : 'Syllogismus ex propositionibus constat, propositiones ex verbis, verba notionum tesserae sunt. Itaque si notiones ipsae (id quod basis rei est) confusae sint, et temere a rebus abstractae; nihil in iis, quae superstruuntur, est firmitudinis. Itaque spes est una in inductione vera.' 'Nec minor est libido et aberratio in constituendis axiomatibus, quam in notionibus abstrahendis; idque in ipsis principiis, quae ab inductione vulgari pendent. At multo major est in axiomatibus et propositionibus inferioribus, quae educit syllogismus.' Unless we make sure of the truth of our first principles at starting, the application of the syllogism may only result in multiplying error instead of deducing truth.

With what Locke here says on the carelessness of men in admitting unproved 'First Principles,' compare the admirable chapter on 'Wrong Assent or Error' in the Essay, Bk. IV, ch. 20, especially §§ 8-10.

Page 17. *in another place.* See Essay, Bk. IV, ch. 12, §§ 12, 13. Cp. Bacon, Novum Organum, Bk. I, Aph. 48 : ' Gliscit intellectus humanus, neque consistere aut acquiescere potis est, sed ulterius petit.' Bacon, thinking of ultimate causes, which he regards as not ascertainable, adds, ' at frustra.' Counselling the encouragement of curiosity on one side, and the cultivation of modesty on the other, he concludes the Aphorism by saying : ' Est autem aeque imperiti et leviter philosophantis, in maxime universalibus causam requirere, ac in subordinatis et subalternis causam non desiderare.'

hypothesis. The word 'hypothesis' seems to be used here not so much in the sense of an assumption, as of a basis or foundation, a sense more akin to the original meaning of the term. Cp. Plato, Republic, p. 511 B: τὰς ὑποθέσεις ποιούμενος οὐκ ἀρχάς, ἀλλὰ τῷ ὄντι ὑποθέσεις, οἷον ἐπιβάσεις τε καὶ ὁρμάς. Plato, however, is speaking of the bases on which we may rise to more general truths, Locke of the general principles on which we 'bottom' our particular beliefs. The former is thinking of the 'bases' of inductive, the latter of the 'bases' of deductive reasoning.

On 'scientific hypothesis' and the circumstances which distinguish it from unscientific hypothesis, see my Inductive Logic, ch. 2, § 3, 5th ed. pp. 97-123.

Page 18. *interest or fancy.* Cp. Essay, Bk. IV, ch. 20, § 12.

Page 19. *more fully.* See the next section.

Page 20. *better than mathematics.* To cultivate habits of precise reasoning, and to train the mind to deal with abstract ideas and principles, no discipline can be better adapted than that of mathematics. But a mind trained exclusively on mathematics would be very ill equipped to deal with the various and complicated problems of life and science. An early training in mathematical reasoning should always be supplemented, as education proceeds, by forming a habit of analysing and estimating the value of evidence in subjects which admit not only of certain, but of more or less probable conclusions, such as language, law, the moral and physical sciences, history, and the affairs of ordinary life.

† *at* † *all rational.* This is the reading of the original edition.

I

But, in the edition of 1781, it is printed as 'not all rational,' which, it seems to me, is much more likely to be what Locke wrote. The 'they' must refer to 'men,' not 'conclusions.'

of reasoning well in others. This remark is not only true, but eminently useful and instructive. 'Natural incapacity' for particular branches of study, say mathematics or language, rarely exists, except in imagination; unless indeed the subject of it is deficient in mental power generally.

Page 21. *have governed all their thoughts.* Men should be peculiarly on their guard against constantly repeating, to themselves or others, compact and neatly-worded maxims. Principles of this kind come after a time to exercise a tyranny over the mind, recur on every occasion, and, being taken without any qualification, often have a wonderful effect in perverting the judgment. The tendency to be constantly enunciating and acting on maxims of this kind is often particularly observable in old men, or persons whose experience has been mainly confined to some one sphere of activity, such as seafaring men or lawyers.

Page 22. *with young scholars.* Locke speaks from experience. Not only had he given much advice with respect to the education of children and young men, but he had spent a great part of his time in the practical work of instruction. In early life he acted as Tutor and Censor of Christ Church. Afterwards, he was instructor to the second, and supervised the studies of the third, Earl of Shaftesbury. Moreover, while in France during the years 1677 and 1678, he travelled with a pupil, the son of a rich merchant named Sir John Banks. It is curious, when we remember Locke's attacks on the logic of the Schools, to learn the nature of his objections to entering young Banks in the study of mathematics. 'To engage one in mathematics who is not yet acquainted with the very rudiments of logic is a method of study I have not known practised, and seems to me not very reasonable.' Letter to Sir John Banks, quoted in Fox-Bourne's Life of Locke, vol. i. p. 378.

SECTION VII.

Page 23. *transfer it.* But, in doing so, they must recollect that they are, for the most part, dealing with propositions which admit only of probable, not of demonstrative, proof.

as in demonstrative knowledge. What Locke means is that the mode of proof, that is, the analysis of the reasoning, is the same in all cases, though in some cases the conclusions may be demonstrative, in others only probable. The only differences which he recognises between demonstrative and probable reasoning are that, in the one, a single proof is sufficient to establish the conclusion, which may then be taken for certain, whereas, in the other, several arguments of varying degrees of probability, some tending one way and some another, have to be taken into account, the conclusion expressing the preponderance of the evidence. For his remarks on Probability, see Essay, Bk. IV, chs. 15, 16, and ch. 17, § 5.

It is by no means correct to say that 'in all sorts of reasoning every single argument should be managed as a mathematical demonstration.' It is indeed true that, in all cases, a belief should be traced 'to the source on which it bottoms' or that the propositions on which our assent is based should be so put together that we may see their connexion with the conclusion. But this connexion may be exhibited in various ways. Thus, the best and most natural mode of representing an inductive argument (see the first chapter of my Elements of Inductive Logic) is entirely different from that of representing a deductive argument, though, by a certain amount of manipulation, the one form may be brought under the other. Again, even in deductive ratiocination, there are rules, quite distinct from those of the ordinary syllogism, for estimating the precise value to be attached to probable arguments, whether in single syllogisms or in combinations of syllogisms or on a balance of rival probabilities. The student will find a statement and discussion of such rules in almost any recent work on Logic. Mr. Venn's Logic of Chance is specially appropriated to the discussion of these and kindred subjects.

disputing in the schools. What Locke thought of the 'disputations,' which were then in common use throughout the universities of Europe, may be gathered from the following passage, which occurs in the 'Thoughts concerning Education,' § 189: 'If the use and end of right reasoning be to have right notions and a right judgment of things, to distinguish betwixt truth and falsehood, right and wrong, and to act accordingly, be sure not to let your son be bred up in the art and formality of disputing, either practising it himself or admiring it in others, unless, instead of an able man, you desire to have him an insignificant wrangler, opinionater in discourse, and priding himself in contradicting others, or—which is worse—questioning everything, and thinking there is no such thing as truth to be sought, but only victory in disputing. There cannot be anything so disingenuous, so misbecoming a gentleman or any one who pretends to be a rational creature, as not to yield to plain reason and the conviction of clear arguments. Is there anything more inconsistent with civil conversation, and the end of all debate, than not to take an answer, though never so full and satisfactory, but still to go on with the dispute as long as equivocal sounds can furnish a *medius terminus*, a term to wrangle with on the one side or a distinction on the other, whether pertinent or impertinent, sense or nonsense, agreeing with or contrary to what he had said before, it matters not? For this, in short, is the way and perfection of logical disputes, that the opponent never take any answer nor the respondent never yield to any argument. This neither of them must do, whatever becomes of truth or knowledge, unless he will pass for a poor baffled wretch, and lie under the disgrace of not being able to maintain whatever he has once affirmed, which is the great aim and glory of disputing.'

one topical argument. Cp. Essay, Bk. IV, ch. 17, § 5.

The expression 'topical argument' applies to an argument derived from certain general heads of probability, which, in the language of Aristotle and his followers, were called τόποι, common places, or common forms. They were the main subject of the art entitled τοπική or διαλεκτική, and of the eight (or, including the Sophistici Elenchi, the nine) books called the Topics. This work deals with logic when applied to disputation on disputable (probable) matter, as opposed to the logic of demonstration in science, which is treated in the Posterior Analytics.

It does not seem to be essential to disputation that only *one* argument should be insisted on, though, of course, by changing his ground, the disputant acknowledges himself to have been defeated on the ground which he originally assumed; or, at least, shows that he has not entire confidence in it.

Page 25. *out of the reckoning.* Here Locke has undoubtedly hit on one of the great excellences of mathematical discipline. The power of abstracting the mind from all irrelevant data and issues is specially developed even by such elementary departments of mathematical work as those of solving what are called 'Problems' in

Algebraic Equations and ' Deductions' in Plane Geometry. Exercises of this kind ought to form an invariable element in early
education. The tendency to dwell on or diverge to irrelevant
topics is, perhaps, the most frequent of all the intellectual faults
to which ordinary men are subject, whether in argument, in conversation, or in thinking for themselves.

as it were in the lump. Instead of reasoning in the lump, they
ought carefully to distinguish the various questions to be resolved,
thus ascertaining exactly where the difficulties lie. When the
various questions have been disentangled, they ought to form a
separate conclusion on each of the questions or groups of questions
before them.

SECTION VIII.

Page 26. *understand and reason right.* It must be recollected
that Locke was himself a writer on religious topics. In 1695, about
two years before he had begun to write the treatise here re-published,
he published his work on ' The Reasonableness of Christianity as
delivered in the Scriptures,' wherein he attempts to discriminate
between the essential and non-essential elements in Christian belief.
During the last years of his life, he was engaged in writing notes on
some of St. Paul's Epistles, which, however, were not published till
after his death. See ch. 9 of my ' Locke' in the series of English
Men of Letters.

Page 27. *in a right way to this knowledge.* I have noticed in
the Introduction that this book was never revised by its author, and
hence that many of the sentences are ungrammatical. In this sentence he must have meant to say, ' and if those who had other idle
hours would only enter them (viz. those who have not), according to
their several capacities, in a right way to this knowledge.'

of the reformed religion. Locke had probably seen and heard a
good deal of the Huguenots during his stay at Montpellier and his
journeys in the south of France. Moreover, the Revocation of the
Edict of Nantes, in 1685, had brought over to England large numbers
of them, who were remarkable for their industry, thrift, and intelli-
gence. It will be noticed that he says ' lately,' referring to the time
before the Revocation of the Edict of Nantes, which had caused such
a large proportion of the French Protestants to emigrate to foreign
countries.

Locke's observations, during his travels, of the intense poverty of the French peasantry are given both in Lord King's Life, and in that of Mr. Fox-Bourne. See the latter, vol. i. pp. 400–402, or my 'Locke,' p. 29.

SECTION IX.

Page 29. *agreement or disagreement of those ideas.* This is the doctrine of the Fourth Book of Locke's Essay. See Bk IV, ch. 1.

SECTION X.

Page 30. *with their eyes.* The word 'their' is emphatic.

Page 31. *haud aequus fuerit.*

'Qui statuit aliquid parte inaudita altera,
Aequum licet statuerit, haud aequus fuit.'

Seneca, Medea, 199, 200.

SECTION XI.

Page 32. *Examine.* This section should have been headed 'Examination.'

Page 35. *in the future course of his life.* This is the ideal of a liberal education, the object of which is to form intellectual aptitudes rather than to infuse specific knowledge. The advocates of a special education, on the other hand, maintain that, after a certain period in a young man's life, the best mode of enabling him to learn well any subject to which he may hereafter apply himself is to exercise him thoroughly on some one branch of knowledge. Lastly, what is called an useful education is one which is designed solely with a view to fitting the pupil for his future profession or walk in life. Locke's point of view is at least as old as the time of Plato. See Republic, p. 518 B, &c., and the whole scheme of the higher education as delineated in that dialogue.

The same view is presented in Locke's Thoughts concerning Education, in a somewhat exaggerated form, so as to be fairly open, perhaps, to the charge of recommending a merely superficial education:

'The great work of a Governor is to fashion the carriage and form the mind; to settle in his pupil good habits and the principles of virtue and wisdom; to give him by little and little a view of mankind, and work him into a love and imitation of what is excellent and praise-worthy; and, in the prosecution of it, to give him vigour, activity, and industry. The studies, which he sets him upon, are but as it were the exercises of his faculties and employment of his time, to keep him from sauntering and idleness, to teach him application, and accustom him to take pains, and to give him some little taste of what his own industry must perfect. For who expects that, under a tutor, a young gentleman should be an accomplished critic, orator, or logician; go to the bottom of Metaphysics, Natural Philosophy, or Mathematics; or be a master in History or Chronology? Though something of each of these is to be taught him. But it is only to open the door, that he may look in and as it were begin an acquaintance, but not to dwell there. And a Governor would be much blamed, that should keep his pupil too long and lead him too far in most of them. But of good breeding, knowledge of the world, virtue, industry, and a love of reputation, he cannot have too much. And, if he have these, he will not long want what he needs or desires of the other.' § 94. He seems, however, immediately to lapse into recommending a merely useful education. ' And since it cannot be hoped he should have time and strength to learn all things, most pains should be taken about that which is most necessary, and that principally looked after, which will be of most and frequentest use to him in the world.' Then, after speaking of the time devoted to learning the technicalities of Logic, he adds : ' Reason, if consulted with, would advise that their children's time should be spent in acquiring what might be useful to them when they come to be men, rather than to have their heads stuffed with a deal of trash, a great part whereof they usually never do ('tis certain they never need to) think on again as long as they live.'

SECTION XIII.

Page 36. *to draw from them conclusions.* The conclusions being inductions, which are based on the facts. Here, again, the spirit of Locke's remarks is thoroughly Baconian.

from every particular they meet with. Cp. Bacon, Novum Organum, Bk. I, Aph. 95 : ' Qui tractaverunt scientias aut empirici aut dogmatici fuerunt. Empirici, formicae more, congerunt tantum, et utuntur : rationales, aranearum more, telas ex se conficiunt : apis vero ratio media est, quae materiam ex floribus horti et agri elicit ; sed tamen eam propria facultate vertit et digerit. Neque absimile philosophiae verum opificium est ; quod nec mentis viribus tantum aut praecipue nititur, neque ex historia naturali et mechanicis

experimentis praebitam materiam, in memoria integram, sed in intel-
lectu mutatam et subactam, reponit. Itaque ex harum facultatum
(experimentalis scilicet et rationalis) arctiore et sanctiore foedere
(quod adhuc factum non est) bene sperandum est.'

Page 37. *of history.* We must recollect that the word *history*
was at this time used for a collection of facts of any kind. Bacon
commonly uses the term in this sense. Thus the alternative title of
the Sylva Sylvarum is 'A Natural History,' and the third part of the
Instauratio Magna was to be entitled 'Phaenomena Universi, sive
Historia Naturalis et Experimentalis ad condendam Philosophiam.'
In the title of Aristotle's work, the Historia Animalium (Περὶ τὰ ζῷα
ἱστορίαι), the word means ' enquiry,' but it quickly passes from this
meaning to signify the result of such an enquiry, the information thus
obtained.

pudder, to confuse, throw up a dust round. The more ordinary term
is *pother* (from poudre, dust). Both words are used alike as substan-
tives and verbs. Thus in the Essay, Bk. III, ch. 5, § 16, Locke says,
'When it is considered, what a pudder is made about essences,' &c.

SECTION XIV.

Page 38. *or themselves for his sake.* Cp. Bacon's Advancement
of Learning, Book I, Aldis Wright's edition, p. 9: 'And as for the
conceit that too much knowledge should incline a man to atheism,
and that the ignorance of second causes should make a more devout
dependence upon God, which is the first cause; first, it is good to
ask the question which Job asked of his friends: *Will you lie for
God, as one man will do for another, to gratify him?* For certain it
is that God worketh nothing in nature but by second causes: and
if they would have it otherwise believed, it is mere imposture, as it
were in favour towards God; and nothing else but to offer to the
author of truth the unclean sacrifice of a lie.'

SECTION XV.

Page 39. *And* [*tt*]. I have ventured to attempt to reconstruct
this and the next sentence.

light. lit or lighted.

those determined ideas. This is the doctrine expounded at large
in the third and fourth books of the Essay.

Page 40. *implicit knowledge.* That is, knowledge which he has merely taken on trust, second-hand knowledge which he has never verified for himself.

SECTION XVI.

Page 41. *jump to the conclusion.* This procedure is what Bacon calls 'anticipatio mentis.'

opiniatrity. This word, which is also used in Sect. 26, means obstinacy in maintaining one's own opinion. It is but slightly altered from the French word opiniâtreté. Sometimes it is spelt *opiniatry. Opinionativeness* is now the more common form.

SECTION XIX.

Page 43. *and that will become everything.* Cp. Bacon, Novum Organum, Bk. I, Aph. 54: 'Adamant homines scientias et contemplationes particulares; aut quia authores et inventores se earum credunt; aut quia plurimum in illis operae posuerunt, iisque maxime assueverunt. Hujusmodi vero homines, si ad philosophiam et contemplationes universales se contulerint, illas ex prioribus phantasiis detorquent, et corrumpunt; id quod maxime conspicuum cernitur in Aristotele, qui naturalem suam philosophiam logicae suae prorsus mancipavit, ut eam fere inutilem et contentiosam reddiderit. Chemicorum autem genus, ex paucis experimentis fornacis, philosophiam constituerunt phantasticam, et ad pauca spectantem: quinetiam Gilbertus, postquam in contemplationibus magnetis se laboriosissime exercuisset, confinxit statim philosophiam consentaneam rei apud ipsum praepollenti.'

Page 44. *and Mercury.* This was the Triad of Paracelsus, and, at an earlier time, of Basilius Valentinus. See my edition of Bacon's Novum Organum, note 45 on Bk. II, Aph. 50, 2nd ed. pp. 587, 8.

SECTION XX.

Page 46. *mizmaze.* A maze or labyrinth. The word is duplicated, for the sake of emphasis.

SECTION XXI.

Page 47. *intermediate principles.* These are those 'axiomata media' of which Bacon speaks, when he says: 'At media sunt axiomata illa vera et solida et viva, in quibus humanae res et fortunae sitae sunt.' Nov. Org. Bk. I, Aph. 104. They may be arrived at in two ways: either by an induction, through the 'axiomata infima,' from particulars; or by deduction from the 'suprema et generalissima axiomata,' only that, in this latter case, the higher axioms themselves must previously have been constituted as the result of a careful induction. Both Locke and Bacon give good advice, when they recommend men, as a general rule, not to run back their conclusions to first principles, but to be content with showing their dependence on nearer and intermediate principles, provided that these last be such as themselves admit of satisfactory proof. When men begin by enunciating some general and abstract principle, and then attach to it the particular conclusion which they wish us to receive, we may reasonably suspect that the intermediate links are wanting, and, any way, we should insist on having them supplied. On the other hand, the connection between the ultimate conclusion and the intermediate principle is often pretty obvious, and the intermediate principle may be one which most men, having any acquaintance with the subject, recognise as not itself requiring proof. The demonstrations in geometry are well cited by Locke as instances in point.

SECTION XXII.

Page 48. *partiality to studies.* This section has much in common with the latter half of Section 19, 'On Universality.'

SECTION XXIII.

Page 50. *words of revelation.* He is here thinking of the distinction between natural and revealed religion, a distinction so much dwelt on by writers in the 17th and 18th centuries.

SECTION XXIV.

Page 51. *chymistry.* Cp. what Locke here says with Sections 19, 22.

Satyrs. Or, as the word would now be written, Satires. The Latin word is Satura or Satira, *not* Satyra, which is an incorrect form. The allusion must be to the Epistles, Bk. II, Ep. 1. The Epistles have often been regarded as continuations of the Satires.

giants. A recent writer, Mr. Goldwin Smith, has somewhere remarked that we have measured the bones of these giants, and found them to be of the same length as our own.

Page 52. *mould and rottenness.* Cp. Bacon, Nov. Org. Bk. I,

Aph. 56: 'Reperiuntur ingenia alia in admirationem antiquitatis, alia in amorem et amplexum novitatis effusa; pauca vero ejus temperamenti sunt, ut modum tenere possint, quin aut quae recte posita sunt ab antiquis convellant, aut ea contemnant quae recte afferuntur a novis. Hoc vero magno scientiarum et philosophiae detrimento fit, quum studia potius sint antiquitatis et novitatis, quam judicia: veritas autem non a felicitate temporis alicujus, quae res varia est; sed a lumine naturae et experientiae, quod aeternum est, petenda est. Itaque abneganda sunt ista studia; et videndum, ne intellectus ab illis ad consensum abripiatur.' ·

less true or less genuine. Bacon (Novum Organum, Bk. I, Aph. 84) has some extremely striking remarks on the exaggerated love for antiquity, though it must be confessed that his own tendency was to err in the direction of unduly depreciating the merits of previous authors:

'Rursus vero homines a progressu in scientiis detinuit et fere incantavit reverentia antiquitatis, et virorum, qui in philosophia magni habiti sunt, authoritas, atque deinde consensus. Atque de consensu superius dictum est.

'De antiquitate autem opinio, quam homines de ipsa fovent, negligens omnino est, et vix verbo ipsi congrua. Mundi enim senium et grandaevitas pro antiquitate vere habenda sunt; quae temporibus nostris tribui debent, non juniori aetati mundi, qualis apud antiquos fuit. Illa enim aetas, respectu nostri, antiqua et major; respectu mundi ipsius, nova et minor fuit. Atque revera quemadmodum majorem rerum humanarum notitiam et maturius judicium ab homine sene expectamus quam a juvene, propter experientiam et rerum, quas vidit, et audivit, et cogitavit, varietatem et copiam; eodem modo et a nostra aetate (si vires suas nosset, et experiri et intendere vellet) majora multo quam a priscis temporibus expectari par est; utpote aetate mundi grandiore, et infinitis experimentis et observationibus aucta et cumulata.

'Neque pro nihilo aestimandum, quod per longinquas navigationes et peregrinationes (quae seculis nostris increbuerunt) plurima in natura patuerint, et reperta sint, quae novam philosophiae lucem immittere possint. Quin et turpe hominibus foret, si globi materialis tractus, terrarum videlicet, marium, astrorum, nostris temporibus immensum aperti et illustrati sint; globi autem intellectualis fines inter veterum inventa et angustias cohibeantur.

'Authores vero quod attinet, summae pusillanimitatis est authoribus infinita tribuere, authori autem authorum, atque adeo omnis authoritatis, Tempori, jus suum denegare. Recte enim Veritas Temporis filia dicitur, non Authoritatis. Itaque mirum non est, si fascina ista antiquitatis et authorum et consensus hominum virtutem ita ligaverint, ut cum rebus ipsis consuescere (tanquam maleficiati) non potuerint.'

The reader may consult my notes, and the various parallel passages which I have cited, in illustration of this Aphorism. See my edition of the Novum Organum, 2nd ed. pp. 282-4.

Page 54. *artificial manner*. The distinction here drawn is that between observation and experiment. In my Inductive Logic (ch. 2, § 1), I have distinguished between these processes as follows: ' To *observe* is to watch with attention phenomena as they occur, to *experiment* (or, to adopt more ordinary language, to *perform an experiment*) is, not only to observe, but also to place the phenomena under peculiarly favourable circumstances, as a preliminary to observation. Thus, every experiment implies an observation, but it also implies something more. In an experiment, I arrange or create the circumstances under which I wish to make my observation. Thus, if two bodies are falling to the ground, and I attend to the phenomenon, I am said to *observe* it ; but, if I place the bodies under the exhausted receiver of an air-pump, or cause them to be dropped under any special circumstances whatever, I may be said not only to make an observation, but also to perform an experiment. Bacon has not inaptly compared experiment with the torture of witnesses. Mr. Mill distinguishes between the two processes, by saying that in observation we *find* our instance in nature, in experiment we *make* it by an artificial arrangement of circumstances.'

Page 56. *can be imputed*. Here again we have an unrevised sentence, which cannot be construed grammatically. The sentence might, perhaps, be recast thus : ' There are not seldom to be found even amongst such as aim . . . men who make,' &c.

of that author's opinions. Hallam, somewhere in his Introduction to the Literature of Europe, says, speaking, I think, of the writers of the 17th century, that they read too many books and entertained too great a respect for their authors.

upon authorities. On the illegitimate employment of the Argument from Authority, see my Inductive Logic, ch. 6, 5th ed. pp. 291-298.

Page 57. *beholding*. ? beholden.

SECTION XXV.

Page 58. *savanas.* Spanish, *sabana.* The word is now usually spelt *savannah.* It is used in those parts of America which are or have been Spanish, to express what is elsewhere called a *prairie,* that is, a tract of land covered with natural vegetation.

Page 59. *whereon to found those general axioms.* Here again Locke is on ground thoroughly familiar to the readers of the Novum Organum. See, for instance, amongst many other places, Bk. I, Aphs. 19-26. There can be no doubt that Locke is indebted to Bacon both for the thought and language of this passage. Cp., for instance, the following sentences in Aphs. 25, 24: 'Axiomata, quae in usu sunt, ex tenui et manipulari experientia, et paucis particularibus, quae ut plurimum occurrunt, fluxere; et sunt fere ad mensuram eorum facta et extensa: ut nil mirum sit, si ad nova particularia non ducant.' 'Sed axiomata, a particularibus rite et ordine abstracta, nova particularia rursus facile indicant et designant.'

Page 60. *suggest hints of enquiry.* Or, in more technical language, may suggest hypotheses or provisional explanations. One or two instances may often put us on the scent, and lead us to some provisional theory, which further enquiry may either confirm, modify, or disprove. A hypothesis, started on these slender grounds, should always be held loosely, and we should constantly be on the look-out for further facts bearing upon it, whether favourable or unfavourable. What, however, frequently happens is that, when a hypothesis has been once formed, all the facts which support it are carefully noted, while those which are unfavourable to it are ignored.

as has been already remarked. See Section 13, and cp. Section 20. Locke's meaning in this sentence is not very clear. The clause beginning 'To make such observations' seems to allude to the habit of merely collecting particulars without basing conclusions on them, whereas the clause beginning 'and he that makes everything an observation' seems to allude to the habit of generalising on insufficient data.

SECTION XXVI.

Page 61. *anticipations of their minds.* Cp. Bacon's expression 'anticipationes mentis.'

opiniatrity. See note on Section 16.

SECTION XXVIII.

Page 62. *recusent.* Horace, Ars Poetica, ll. 39, 40:

> ' Et versate diu, quid ferre recusent,
> Quid valeant humeri.'

Page 64. *that dignity.* There is a play on this word. Dignitas is one of the synonyms for axiom. This use of the word goes back as far as the times of Priscian and Boethius, while Latin was still a living language.

well beaten track. That is, who think it a sufficient excuse for going astray, if the wrong path they take be a well beaten track.

SECTION XXIX.

Page 64. *in another place.* That is, the Third Book of the Essay, and especially ch. 10.

Page 65. *substantial forms and intentional species.* The *substantial form* was regarded as that occult principle which, actuating, as it were, matter, produced the distinctive manifestations of any particular class of Substances. Chauvin (Lexicon Philosophicum) gives the following account of the Peripatetic doctrine of *substantial forms :* 'Peripatetici formam definiunt per rationem Substantiae, seu rationem talem, per quam res aliqua certa ac determinata substantia evadit, atque est. Ex materia prima et forma substantiali compositum substantiale fieri volunt. Alias illam definiunt per substantiam incompletam, quae materiae unita corpus naturale componit, omniumque hujus operationum primum principium est, certis tamen qualitatibus tanquam instrumentis utitur ad suos effectus producendos. Scilicet in quovis corpore, post materiam illam primam, quam fingunt, praeter extensionem solidam seu impenetrabilem, praeterque omnia accidentia sensibilia, formam aliquam substantialem sensibus occultam, caeterarum dominam, inexistere, cui in omnibus functionibus hae ministrent, indubitanter asserunt.' Thus, the 'rational soul' (anima rationalis) is the 'substantial form' of man.

Intentional Species were supposed to be certain images or similitudes intermediate between the outward object and the percipient mind. They *represented* to the mind, it was thought, the various qualities as they existed in the object. They were called *species* (εἴδη), that is, forms or appearances, because they were regarded as representative of the external reality ; *intentional* (from *intentio animi*), that is, notional, in order to distinguish them from material and wholly objective appearances. They were supposed to be neither merely affections of external objects nor merely modifications of the mind, but a something mediating between mind and matter, and thus enabling the former to become acquainted with the latter. On this conception, and on the distinction between sensible and intelligible species, species impressae and species expressae, see Hamilton's Reid, pp. 952-957. It must be acknowledged that traces of this doctrine are to be found even in Locke's Essay; for he sometimes seems to speak of 'ideas,' as if they were not merely mental modifications, but a tertium quid, a something intermediate between external objects and the mind. See, for instance, Essay, Bk. II, ch. 1, § 25 ; Bk. IV, ch. 21, § 4.

insignificant. That is, non-significant, having no meaning.

etch out. That is, to complete, to fill in the outline of their systems.

I know not what. Locke constantly speaks in the Essay of the idea of Substance as of a 'something I know not what.' The remark in the Text, it is almost needless to point out, affords a good instance of Locke's felicitous way of stating homely truths.

Page 66. *simple ones.* See Essay, Bk. II, chs. 1, 2.

SECTION XXX.

Page 67. *from straggling.* Cp. the Sections (123-127) on Sauntering, in the Thoughts concerning Education.

SECTION XXXI.

Page 68. *Distinction and division.* If Locke uses these terms in their proper sense, they may be distinguished as follows. A *distinction* is a determination of the various meanings of an equivocal term, such as canis, humanity, post, &c. (and, in practice, it was extended to determining the various meanings of ambiguous sentences). A *division*, in the strict sense of the word, is a determination of the various species which fall under the same genus, or, to employ less technical language, of the various subject-classes which fall under the same higher class. It is thus an exposition of what logicians call the denotation of a term. Thus, to distinguish the various meanings of a word like humanity, church, house, &c., would be a *distinction.* To enumerate the various kinds of plane rectilineal

figures, namely, triangles, squares, and polygons, would be a *division*.
' In a distinction the same definition is not predicable of each of the
terms distinguished, but in a division the same definition is predicable
of each dividing member ' (as the subject-classes are called).   See my
Deductive Logic, Part II, ch. 8.

Bishop Sanderson (whose Compendium of Logic was in common
use in Locke's time) thus distinguishes between Distinction and
Division in Pt. I, ch. 18 : ' *Divisio* est latioris in angustiora deductio.
Quae si sit *nominis*, *distinctio*, si *rei*, *Divisio* magis proprie appellatur.
Distinctio est ambiguae vocis in sua significata distributio : ut canis
in piscem, domesticum animal, et coeleste sidus.   Ambiguum omne
prius est distinguendum, quam definiendum ; indistinctio enim parit
continuas lites : nec aliter constabit, quid aut de quo agatur.   Nec
tamen semper excutiendae sunt omnes significationum minutiae,
sed quae sunt cum subjecto negotio conjunctae, aut in quibus error
contingere potest, si non distinguantur.—*Divisio rei perfecta* est
totius alicujus proprie dicti in partes proprie dictas distributio.'   He
then proceeds to explain what is a whole and what are parts, properly so called ; the one being a genus, or logical whole, the other
being species, or logical parts.   Chauvin (Lexicon Philosophicum)
says : ' Distinctio Logica simia est divisionis.   In hoc loco divisi,
consistit vocabulum homonymum ; et loco membrorum dividentium,
plures termini, qui isto vocabulo significantur.   V. g. sentiens aliud
actu, aliud potentia sentit.'

Locke's meaning in this Section is not always very clear, but I
cannot doubt that what he intends to commend is *Division*, ' the
perception of a difference that nature has placed in things,' while
what he wishes to caution his readers against is over-subtlety in
Distinction.   The determination of the various subject-classes which
are included under any higher class, like the reverse process of
grouping lower classes under some higher class (' generalisation '),
is a logical process indispensable to any complicated act of reasoning.
Any man who can analyse his thoughts will find that he is performing
both these processes all day long.   Distinction is also a process of
the greatest utility, but it is not employed to nearly the same extent
as division, and, if words and sentences were properly constructed,
it would not be required at all.   We must recollect, in reading this
Section, that Locke has an eye to the ' Disputations,' which were so
common in the Universities in his time, the method of which largely

affected the controversial, and especially the theological, writings of his contemporaries. In these disputations, the distinctions were often of the most frivolous and shadowy character, being, in fact, 'distinctions without differences.' It is against the waste of time and 'puzzling of the understanding' involved in such useless and over-subtle distinctions that Locke is here mainly protesting, though it cannot escape his notice that the process of division may similarly be over-strained, either by recognising too minute shades of difference in constituting the subject-classes or by needlessly increasing the number of steps in the descending process of sub division. Hence, a certain amount of confusion is produced in this Section by considering together, and apparently not always carefully distinguishing between, the two faults of over-subtlety in distinction and over-minuteness in division. Both of these faults were more common in Locke's time than in our own, but they are still common enough to render the warnings of this section not altogether superfluous to the modern reader.

Page 69. *thereby one from another.* That is to say, there would no longer be any need of distinctions, but there would still be need of divisions.

Page 70. *too much.* 'Distinguo' is the constantly recurring term of the scholastic disputations.

Page 71. *they are right.* That is, the verbal distinctions.

Page 72. *conceptions of them.* On the tendency of the mind to note differences rather than resemblances, or resemblances rather than differences, one of the instances of the *idola specus*, there is an admirable aphorism in the Novum Organum : 'Maximum et velut radicale discrimen ingeniorum, quoad philosophiam et scientias, illud est : quod alia ingenia sint fortiora et aptiora ad notandas rerum differentias ; alia, ad notandas rerum similitudines. Ingenia enim constantia et acuta figere contemplationes, et morari, et haerere in omni subtilitate differentiarum possunt ; ingenia autem sublimia et discursiva etiam tenuissimas et catholicas rerum similitudines et agnoscunt et componunt : utrumque autem ingenium facile labitur in excessum, prensando aut gradus rerum, aut umbras.'—Nov. Org. Bk. I, Aph. 55.

SECTION XXXII.

Page 72. *think aright.* A simile or metaphor may often be most appropriately used for the purpose of illustrating or enforcing

K

an argument, but it should never be used in lieu of an argument. 'How does this simile apply to the case in point, and what is the argument which it is meant to illustrate,' are questions which should always be asked, when a simile, metaphor, or allegory is employed. From want of putting these questions, men often deceive, not only others, but themselves.

Page 73. *under consideration.* This sentence is somewhat involved. The emphatic word in it is *only*. 'Which' refers to the 'borrowed representations' and 'foreign ideas.'

SECTION XXXIII.

Page 74. *to give assent.* The student should read the chapters on Probability and Degrees of Assent in the Essay. See Bk. IV, chs. 15, 16.

all as uncertain. Like the two ancient sects of the New Academy and the Ephectici (Pyrrhonists or Sceptics).

SECTION XXXIV.

Page 75. *said above.* See Section 11, which is on the same subject as this.

Page 77. *born to orthodoxy.* Orthodoxy, which, according to the original usage of the term, is the dogma of the Catholic Church as opposed to the tenets of heretics, is, practically speaking, at any particular time and in any particular country, the body of opinions then and there most prevalent.

Page 78. *best state of the three.* The reader will be reminded, though the cases are not strictly parallel, of the answer of the Delphic Oracle to Chaerephon, that there was no man wiser than Socrates, and of Socrates' explanation of the response, that he alone was conscious of his own ignorance. The conceit of knowledge without the reality was a far inferior state of mind to ignorance with the consciousness of it. See Plato's Apology of Socrates, and Grote's Greece, Pt. II, ch. 68.

SECTION XXXV.

Page 79. *or chymists.* These were various sects of physicians. The Dogmatists and Empirics were opposed rather in respect of their logical method than their medical doctrine. The former, who trusted mainly to the deductions of reason, falsely claimed for themselves the authority of Hippocrates (the great physician of Cos, born, according to the common account, B.C. 460) ; the latter, who professed to ground their conclusions solely on experience, may conveniently be dated from Philinus of Cos. who flourished about 250 B.C. The Methodists were a later school, and appear to have meant nothing more by the name which they assumed than that they proposed a new method, distinct from that of either the Dogmatists or Empirics. Their doctrine rested on a philosophical theory of Atomism. Its earliest exponents were Asclepiades of one of the towns named Prusa in Bithynia and Themison of Laodicea, both belonging to the 1st century, B.C. By the 'chymists' Locke probably means the followers of Paracelsus (b. 1493, d. 1541), though 'chymiatria' or the art of healing by means of drugs had, of course, existed long before his time. The body, according to Paracelsus, being composed of sulphur, mercury, and salt, all disease arises from the relative increase, diminution, or disarrangement of these elements. For further information on these schools, the reader may consult the History of Medicine of Sprengel, Daremberg, or Bouchut.

SECTION XXXVII.

Page 81. *oscitancy.* Laziness. The Latin word 'oscitatio,' perhaps from 'os' and 'cito' (moving the mouth), means literally 'gaping' or 'yawning,' and, hence, laziness.

SECTION XXXVIII.

Page 82. *Fortunatus' purse.* 'Fortunatus is the legendary hero of one of the most popular of European chap-books. He was a native, says the story, of Famagosta in Cyprus, and after many strange adventures and vicissitudes fell in with the goddess of Fortune in a wild forest, and received from her a purse which was continually replenished as often as he drew from its stores.' . . . 'The earliest known edition of the German text of Fortunatus appeared at Augsburg in 1509, and the modern German investigators are disposed to regard this as the original form. Innumerable rifacimentos have been made in French, Italian, Dutch, English, &c., and cheap editions are still common enough on the bookstalls.' Encyclopaedia Britannica.

SECTION XXXIX.

Page 83. *eundo.* Virg. Aen. iv. 175.

vicere. See Livy, Bk. II, ch. 64: 'Impetu facto, dum se putant vincere, vicere.' Cp. Virg. Aen. v. 231 :

'Hos successus alit: possunt, quia posse videntur.'

Page 86. *said elsewhere.* Cp. Sections 25, 28, and Thoughts concerning Education, Sections 64–66.

unperplexed proposition. This is another sentence, the construction of which would probably have been altered, had the book been revised. As it stands, it is doubtful whether we should take the words from 'simple, unperplexed proposition' to the end of the sentence as an independent clause, the construction then being that of the ablative absolute, or regard them as describing the requisites of the 'next adjoining part yet unknown.' Either way, what is meant by 'simple, unperplexed proposition' is a proposition making one simple statement or asking one simple question, as opposed to a proposition involving a number of statements or asking a plurality of questions, and therefore putting before the mind several issues instead of one.

SECTION XL.

Analogy. On the various meanings of the word Analogy, and on the nature of the argument founded on Analogy, in the modern sense of that term, see my Inductive Logic, ch. 4. The peculiarity of the argument is that we do not draw our inference from a number of instances, as in Induction, but from a number of points of resemblance. 'The argument is based, not on the number of *instances* in which the two sets of qualities are found united, but on the number of *qualities* which are found to be common to two or more instances: the argument is not that I have so often observed *a, b, c* in conjunction with *m* that I believe these qualities to be conjoined invariably, but that I know X and Y to resemble each other in so many points that I believe them to resemble each other in all.' The argument is never absolutely conclusive, because its very characteristic is to argue from a number of known points of resemblance to the common possession of some other quality which is known to exist in the one instance but not known to exist in the other. Were it *known* to exist in both, either as a matter of fact or as a certain inference from induction, there would be no occasion for the argument from analogy.

may be justified. But, if we know that the good effect is owing wholly to the acidity, the argument is not an analogical but an inductive argument, and, wherever we find acidity, unless there be counteracting circumstances, we may be certain that the good effect will follow. On the other hand, if we know that the good effect is *not* owing to the acidity, there is an equally certain induction on the negative side, and no ground for analogy whatever. The very essence of the argument from analogy is that there should be some amount of uncertainty as to whether the quality known to belong to the one case or instance [here the power of producing a good effect] also belongs to the other, and, if we actually know that it is due to some other quality which both the cases or instances possess in common, the argument ceases to be analogical and becomes inductive. See my Inductive Logic, 5th ed. p. 226, &c. It is almost needless to say that the analysis of inductive reasoning, and the discrimination of its various kinds, were little advanced in Locke's time, nor was he, as many passages of the Essay show, at all adequately acquainted even with what had already been done or suggested by Bacon in this department of Logic.

SECTION XLI.

Page 87. *Human Understanding.* See Bk. II, ch. 33. This admirable chapter, which the student should by all means consult, was added in the Fourth Edition of the Essay, published in 1699. It had probably been written some years before.

Page 88. *principling.* That is, imbuing them, by repeated admonition, with general maxims of conduct or general principles of speculation, the truth of which is taken for granted. On 'Principles,' see Section 6.

Page 89. *united in their heads.* That is to say, that ideas come not to be thought to have a necessary or usual connection, when they have no such necessary or usual connection as a matter of fact, and that the extent of any usual connection be not exaggerated.

in another place. He is referring here to the celebrated passage contained in the Essay, Bk. II, ch. 9, §§ 8-10. The reference in § 8 to Mr. Molyneux was inserted in the Second Edition. It would be out of place here to refer at any length to the manner in which this idea was worked out and extended by Bp. Berkeley in his

New Theory of Vision, or to the subsequent developments and modifications of Berkeley's theory by Professor Bain and others. See Berkeley's 'Essay towards a New Theory of Vision,' with Professor Fraser's Preface, and Professor Bain's Mental Science, Bk. II, ch. 7, sections on Theory of Vision. The most familiar and perhaps the best example of 'the change of the ideas of sense into those of judgment' is to be found in the acquired perceptions of sight. Thus, for instance, our estimates of distance are, in the language of Berkeley, formed by 'an act of judgment grounded on experience rather than by sense.' We do not *see* distance, but we learn to estimate it, whether it be near or remote, by constantly repeated acts of comparison between our various visual sensations, on the one hand, and the sensations derived from touch, muscular exertion, and locomotion, on the other.

SECTION XLII.

Page 90. *Fallacies.* In its widest and commonest sense, a Fallacy may be described as any error either in the premises or the conclusions of our arguments. Such errors are due sometimes to moral, sometimes to intellectual causes. One chapter, at least, in every work on Logic, and that which is almost invariably the most practically useful, is devoted to the discussion of Fallacies. See, for instance, Mill's Logic, Bk. V, my Deductive Logic, Pt. III, Ch. 8, and my Inductive Logic, Ch. 6. Bacon's very fresh and interesting treatment of Fallacies is to be found in his doctrine of the Idola, Novum Organum, Bk. I, Aphs. 38-70.

SECTION XLIII.

Page 94. *purely logical enquiries.* That is to say, in mere logical subtleties and technical distinctions. Opposed as Locke was to the logical discipline then prevailing, he would have been one of the last to question the importance of analysing the reasoning process and determining the ultimate grounds on which the various orders of our beliefs rest. To answer these questions was, in fact, one of his main motives for writing the Essay.

Page 95. *Mr. Newton.* Compare what Locke says of Newton in the Epistle to the Reader, prefixed to the Essay: 'The Commonwealth of Learning is not at this time without master-builders, whose mighty designs, in advancing the sciences, will leave lasting